PELICAN BOOKS

A264

PHILHARMONIC

THOMAS RUSSELL

Philharmonic

A FUTURE FOR THE SYMPHONY ORCHESTRA

*

THOMAS RUSSELL

With an Introduction by
J. B. PRIESTLEY

*

Illustrations by
ALAN GREGORY

PENGUIN BOOKS
MELBOURNE · LONDON · BALTIMORE

First published 1942
First published in Penguin Books 1953

Made and Printed in Great Britain
for Penguin Books Ltd
by Hunt, Barnard and Co, Ltd, London and Aylesbury

Contents

Introduction by J.B. Priestley — 7

Author's Note — 13

1 The Evolution of a Modern Orchestra — 18
   (a) Chaos and Experiment
   (b) The Orchestra Emerges
   (c) Recent History

2 Conductorless Orchestras — 42

3 The Leader of the Orchestra — 48

4 Conductors Face to Face — 54

5 Should the Composer Know Best? — 68

6 The Perfect Orchestra — 76

7 A Background to Music — 100

8 Interlude I – Instruments and Players — 104

9 The Problem of the Concert Hall — 113

10 The Building of Programmes — 125

11 Interlude II – On Audiences in General — 135

12 Music Betrayed — 143

13 Interlude III – Gramophone Records — 151

14 Concerts for Children — 160

15 The Finance of a Modern Orchestra — 166

16 Conclusions — 176

Index — 203

'IF ever there is any truth again in the saying that England is an unmusical country, it will be, not that she wraps her talents in a napkin, but that she squanders them. The nineteenth century recovered the national heritage in music; it remains for the twentieth to discover wisdom in its use.'

H. C. COLLES

*Introduction
by J. B. Priestley*

THIS is a book about Symphony Orchestras by a man who has both played in them and managed one of them, the London Philharmonic. As you stared at the black-and-white ranks of players, you must have often wondered, as I know I have often wondered, what the more intelligent of them thought about their profession and its problems. Well, here is the answer. In these chapters you are taken behind, through one of those mysterious curtained entrances and exits, and then, perhaps in a narrow passage-way blue with smoke, are talked to by the orchestra. Not that you could call Thomas Russell – who is an alert, smallish, brownish man with a vivid dark eye – an average orchestral player. If all of them had his energy and pugnacity and intelligence, the history of contemporary English music would be quite different. Besides, no average player could become secretary and business manager of the London Philharmonic. No, our author is well above the average, and very much a character. I recognized this – and trust the recognition was mutual – when we first met, in that fine fateful summer of 1940, to decide what could be done to save the L.P.O. and there and then organized our 'Musical Manifesto' at the Queen's Hall that opened a successful campaign.

Since then the L.P.O., with Thomas Russell never far away, has never stopped playing and travelling, and has introduced symphonic music to hundreds of thousands of good folk who had never heard it before, but are now ready for as much as they can be given. Especially was this true of the badly bombed towns, where often the music arrived not very long after the sealed tins of standard soup and other emergency rations. Any lingering notion that the ordinary folk of this country are not musical and so do not want concerts will not survive half an hour's talk with Thomas Russell or any other member of the L.P.O. The fact is, the people who are not musical in this country are the politicians, both municipal and national; and that is why we notice so many hindrances in the way of making music for the people. I suspect that some of them *hate* music.

A great symphony orchestra must be counted among the country's capital achievements. If you think it is easy to create such an orchestra, just try creating one. Even when you have assembled the necessary eighty or ninety first-class instrumentalists, you are still faced with the task of making a real orchestra out of them. An orchestra develops a life and character of its own. It is not simply so many musicians. The London Philharmonic, the Hallé, the New York Philharmonic, the Boston Symphony, are all magnificent orchestras, but they are all quite different in character. Therefore, you cannot regard one of these orchestras merely as a collection of instrumentalists. You cannot do simple sums with it. If you take away ten from eighty, it does not follow that there will be seventy left, for there might easily be nothing left, no orchestra at all.

And the same applies to its finances. If you make a reduction of ten or twenty per cent in its income on some pretext of economy, the deficit does not merely mean a cutting down of the number of players, or greater efforts on the part of them all. It is more likely to mean the loss of everything we most value in a scramble to remain in existence.

8

And I trust this will meet the eye of the London County Council. Their problem is to make the best use of their splendid new concert hall, which was planned to accommodate a resident orchestra – the L.P.O., we were all led to believe. With a little courage the original scheme can be taken up again, and those members of the London Philharmonic who have been loyal to their ideals for so many years will be given their just reward. Until then, the players will continue to face the incessant travelling, rehearsing, performing, demanded now by a permanent orchestra such as the L.P.O., which travels thousands of miles every year to fulfil all its provincial engagements and lift up the hearts of the people.

I hope that every reader will take careful note of Chapter Nine here, on 'The Problem of the Concert Hall.' This country has always been short of adequate concert halls. It was my good fortune, when I was young, to live in a city, Bradford, that at that time had a reasonably good hall, St George's Hall, in which I heard some of the best music-making of the time at prices of admission I could afford. But for the last twenty years, this hall has not been available for regular concerts, and the musical life of my native city has suffered in consequence. For symphony concerts a hall with good acoustic properties, holding about three thousand persons in comfort, is necessary. We were short of them before the war, and now we are worse off than ever. London has, at last, its own first-class concert hall, but we must wait to assess its contribution to the musical life of the metropolis. As Mr Russell points out, even most of the good halls now available are really much too small. If there is room for only about a thousand people in a hall, then either the prices of admission will be too high or the concert will be run at a loss. And even if arrangements can be made for a guarantee against loss, the result is still unsatisfactory because a great many people have been kept away from the music either by the high prices or by the sheer lack of seats. Therefore, what we urgently need is a series of good concert halls throughout the country. They can, of course, be used for other purposes – meetings, dances, and so forth – but they should be designed and built in the first place for symphony concerts. It is in fact the architects and builders who must set to work to create the necessary conditions for the growth of our musical life.

It is my belief that with an adequate supply of good concert halls and a proper organization of the work of the great orchestras, we could soon make symphonic music pay for itself in this country. Once the nation agreed to support its first-class orchestras, to insure all their members against unemployment or cut salaries, to guarantee some kind of pensions fund too, I believe that within a year or two very little public money would actually be needed and that our musical life would be immensely enriched. There is no doubt whatever that the audiences are there and are rapidly growing. The people want music. They may not want it as impresarios wanted them to have it before the war – that is, at fifteen shillings a seat and in evening dress – but under their own sensible conditions, they certainly want it. And the sooner music is taken out of that atmosphere of preciousness and wealth and fashion, the better it will be for music. What were Bach, Mozart, Beethoven, and Brahms doing in that glittering galley? Once the halls are there, the next thing is to put all the established symphony orchestras – the London Philharmonic and the London Symphony for the capital, the Birmingham for the Midlands, the Hallé for the North, and the Scottish for Scotland – on a sound permanent basis, to insure them against any deficit, and then to set them working as hard as it is possible for an orchestra to work without losing its quality. They should be regarded in the first place as being just as much a part of our national cultural life as our libraries, museums, and picture galleries. They should not have to worry about money but only about the quality of their performances. There has to be good music in this country *whether it pays for itself or not.* (Incidentally, all these arguments apply equally well to first-class drama. I for one have never been able to understand the curious distinction in the Anglo-Saxon mind between literature and art, which have long been subsidized, and music and drama, which are rarely subsidized, and often taxed.) Once this is admitted, and the orchestras are secured against financial disaster, it is my opinion that very soon music of the highest class will be found to be supporting itself. And the national gain will be enormous.

The London Philharmonic, with which Mr Russell was associated, is a self-governing orchestra, and as we might therefore expect, he is strongly in favour of such self-government. There can be little doubt that so far the system has worked admirably with the London Philharmonic. It has seen the orchestra through a very bad time. It has taken the strain well. Whether it is the perfect system is another matter. My own feeling is that in this, as in other enterprises, both artistic and industrial, a carefully balanced combination of self-government with outside guidance and control is the best possible system. After all, even here in music, it is no bad thing if the consumer should be represented too. After a time men in any profession or trade are apt to become extremely conservative-minded and to resent any suggestion of change. In recent years, the London Philharmonic, by establishing an external Council representing a certain amount of that outside guidance and control, has accepted the point I am making; but I must now leave the reader to examine Mr Russell's arguments, which are clearly the product of a lively and courageous intelligence. His book is a contribution to our musical life, and I am sure that a host of readers will soon agree with me, and will be thankful that by some private miracle, during his busy days and nights with his orchestra, he found time to produce these stimulating chapters. And let that be the final chord of this Overture.

Author's Note

When a symphony orchestra files on to the platform of a certain concert hall at a fixed time and date, followed first by the leader, then by the conductor, and settles down to perform a programme of music chosen from the compositions of the last 250 years, members of the audience may sometimes wonder how such a unity of time, place, and intent has been secured. In more tranquil times, such inner questionings may have disturbed the flow of the listener's thoughts but little; the almost fatal mistake of taking things for granted and realizing their value only when they are slipping from our grasp was an outstanding feature of our mentality before 1939. But the dire threat which the war made to the realization of intellectual and aesthetic ideals brought many people to earth, and those responsible for taking music to the many towns of Britain since that time have found a new audience, vitally interested in their art.

At the beginning of the war all our cultural life was at stake; some politicians were saying that to fight the war effectively would mean the sacrifice of all those values which had raised us out of the jungle. In spite of official blindness, symphonic music made gallant and rather spectacular efforts to survive, and those members of the public to whom life was more than a wild scramble for bread and security, or the preservation of privilege, expressed their profound disquietude at the threatened loss of

13

cultural values. Music thus received more than its normal support, and was presented with unprecedented opportunities of development. The breakdown of certain social ties and conditions made it possible to put the best music within the reach of a wide and hitherto neglected public, which immediately displayed a healthy curiosity in all that goes on behind the scenes to make a successful concert possible.

When the journal of the London Philharmonic Orchestra, the *Philharmonic Post*, was first issued early in 1940, it went out to a restricted body of readers, but in a few months an amazing demand became apparent. When later this was followed by the *Hallé* magazine, another from Birmingham, and the *London Symphony Observer*, thousands of readers showed a keen interest in details about the orchestras, about their activities and problems which changing conditions had presented to them, and the manner in which they were attempting to solve them. They were no longer content to regard a concert as a fortuitous combination of circumstances, but began to take the view that they could be more than mere onlookers and auditors of such an event.

My object in presenting the chapters of this book to that new public is to familiarize them as far as possible with all the new ideas which are fermenting behind the ordinary façade of an orchestral concert, to point out to them the insecure foundation on which organized music stands, to express my dissatisfaction with many conditions which have long been taken for granted, and to state as far as my experience will allow the essential lines of development which must be followed if symphonic music in this country is to take its rightful place as an art, an entertainment, and a branch of culture.

Since this new public regards music primarily, and quite rightly, as entertainment, I have kept the book as free from technical matters as was possible, and although it deals with a world with which they may never come into direct contact, I am convinced that any light which I may be able to throw on the most highly organized form of music which we possess will help to enrich their experiences in the concert hall, and lead them to take a more intelligent and critical attitude to all that they hear.

But they have a right to know whether I am likely to prove a satisfactory guide over this difficult ground, and a few biographical details may be of use.

For a number of years I served my apprenticeship as a concert-goer by attending every concert at Queen's Hall which my purse would permit; but to listen from the outside soon ceased to satisfy me, and I became a professional musician. After many years as a violinist and viola player I arrived, having gone through the mixed career of the less outstanding among musicians, in one of the B.B.C. orchestras. From this I graduated into the L.P.O. in 1935, and although I cannot claim the distinction of being a foundation member of this body I shared its experiences long enough to realize that all was not well with the internal or external arrangements of symphony orchestras in England. Before 1939 I had already made vague plans upon my criticisms, but it was not until the war had turned things upside down, and I had taken charge of the business administration of the L.P.O., that I obtained a closer association with these many problems.

These years of work with the L.P.O. have completed a round of experience which enables me to study the symphony orchestra from many angles; they have helped me to see the tremendous possibilities which the present unsettled period is offering us, and the great future which lies ahead if we are shrewd enough to profit by them. It is, of course, inevitable that I should refer frequently to the London Philharmonic Orchestra, and draw most of my illustrations from its experiences, but it must not be thought that this is done to boost that organization, or that I consider it possible for any one orchestra to solve the problems with which the development of symphonic music will face us. The future offers scope for more and better orchestras than the L.P.O., but by the pioneer work which it has undertaken it has proved itself to be the spearhead of future developments, and those responsible for its guidance will be rewarded by the greater part which orchestras and orchestral players will take in the life of the community.

We have grown up to accept a number of labels about ourselves and our country; some of them please, some infuriate, and some merely leave us indifferent. 'Land of Hope and Glory', 'perfide Albion', 'unmusical England', are examples of such epithets. There is perhaps some truth in each of them, but less in the last than in either of the others. How, if we are an unmusical nation, can we have succeeded in building even the small number of excellent orchestras which we have to our credit? How is it that our choirs have gained such a high reputation? How have we reared the list of composers during the past fifty years, whose names and achievements will stand comparison with those of other countries? How, indeed, when there has been an almost complete lack of organization on the part of those responsible for providing our musical fare?

It is this lack of organization alone which has laid us open to the charge of possessing no musical culture. The war showed that when music is offered to the people of England they will accept it as gratefully as the inhabitants of any country, and if we take stock of our talents and exploit them as we have exploited our material possessions and inventive genius, what might not the future hold?

Additional Note to this Edition

ANY book written amidst the excitement of a war is likely to date rapidly, and there might be little justification in reissuing *Philharmonic*, but for the fact that so many of its lessons have still to be learned.

In April 1942, the continued existence of symphony orchestras in this country was a matter of grave doubt, but, succeeding as they did in surmounting the worst threats of disaster, it might have been supposed that now, almost ten years later, their worst troubles would be over. This is far from true. Important advances have indeed been made, but the future is little more certain that it was when I first pointed the dangers which beset us. Periodically, the Hallé Orchestra comes into the news, fighting a notable battle for increased grants and considering itself fortunate when its subsidies are not cut. Other orchestras achieve the miracle of balancing upon the razor edge of solvency by methods which have little relation to art. The London County Council, for obscure reasons hidden behind suave official excuses, suddenly deprives the L.P.O. of assistance which everyone accepted as part of a long-term policy, and the Arts Council of Great Britain vainly attempt to achieve their vision of secure permanent orchestras with totally inadequate means.

In this situation, the problems are no less urgent. In a world from which simple common sense has been almost banished, where the lessons of disaster are already forgotten, the claims of civilization have still to be put forward. I believe that the ordinary man has a pretty sound sense of values, and it was for him that this book was originally conceived. I can only hope that its reappearance may represent one step forward in the advance which we are making towards the sane, civilized world, in which the art of music will continue to be one of man's finest achievements.

MARCH, 1951

I The Evolution of a Modern Orchestra

(a) Chaos and Experiment

WE are so willing to take the existing condition of things for granted that when, for example, we hear a young child sing for the first time we notice that it employs the same scale which is in current use in the Western world and conclude that this scale and this system of tonality are thus proved to be natural phenomena. In doing this, we underestimate hereditary influences and, more certainly, the amazing powers of mental absorption in the child. Because we, in our lifetime, have always thought along certain musical lines, we find it difficult to believe that our predecessors and certain living races did, and still do, base their music upon very different systems. I am reminded of an old French lady I knew, who prided herself upon the fact that, although living in Paris, she never left her own *quartier*, and never went into the centre of the city. She was so convinced that French was the natural tongue of a human being that she would talk away volubly to my wife in that language, and be completely mystified to find that she was making no impression. Secretly, she must have thought my wife incredibly stupid.

In the same way, many of us believe that the orchestra as we know it is the natural, logical, and inevitable medium for symphonic music. We overlook the fact that there is no *absolute* reason why the modern symphony orchestra should

18

be constituted as it is. It has not been proved that sixteen first violins, fourteen seconds, twelve violas, and so on, against three flutes, three oboes, and similar numbers of wood-wind and brass, offer the composer the greatest possible scope. In the early days of the orchestra, when attempts were being made to discover a satisfactory balance between the various sections, it was not unusual to have five oboes and five bassoons in an orchestra of forty instruments or so, and it might be that sixteen oboes, fourteen clarinets, etc., combined with three solo violins and a similar number of strings each given a separate part, would provide a far richer palette for the composer. I say it 'might', for we shall probably never know; the disposition of the modern orchestra, which has remained virtually unchanged for over a century, has had its effect on the relative numbers of music students who have directed their energies towards certain instruments, and we should be hard put to it to find the requisite number of players for such a reconstituted orchestra. The present dearth of bassoon players provides a striking instance of this law of supply and demand. In the many small orchestras which were employed in various places of entertainment before the war, and particularly before the introduction of the sound-film, less sensitive directors of music were prepared to replace the bassoon by the cello. They knew that the compass of the latter instrument was similar to that of the bassoon, that the parts of the two instruments frequently doubled each other, and, regardless of the essential difference of tone-colour, they preferred to engage an instrumentalist who would be more useful for general purposes. Students who might have taken up the bassoon were easily persuaded, therefore, to turn their attention to an instrument which offered them a more assured future. Apart from such reasons, the thing has gone too far now, and even if we thought a change in the balance of the orchestra desirable, it would be a practical impossibility, for almost all the works which we insist on hearing regularly were composed for an orchestra exactly like, or, at least, closely resembling the one we are accustomed to hear to-day. But this does not rule out a further gradual change and development.

Although the modern orchestra might have been organized in quite a different way, its present form is not the result of any arbitrary decision. Like the existing system of scales and keys, it has gone through several stages of development and reached its present, and not necessarily final, form at a comparatively recent date. The modern orchestra has, indeed, such a recent history that one would hesitate to credit it with very much stability. Nothing that could reasonably be compared with the orchestra as we know it existed more than 200 years ago, and if we could go back that short distance in time we should have some surprises, for even then the battle for existence, the struggle for the survival of the fittest among instruments, was still being waged. Far back into history and pre-history stretched the long and irregular line of strange instruments with their pretensions to posterity and, perhaps, immortality. Shawms and rebecs, lutes and viols, recorders, psalteries, pipes and tabors, wooden cornets, serpents, chalumeaus, ophicleides, theorboes, and hunting-horns, all jostled one another in a race to adapt themselves to the demands they had created and which were now running ahead of them. Many disappeared or became museum-pieces, others more susceptible of development moved along by easy stages, and others again gave rise to new instruments which bore little likeness to the originals. Between the demands of progressive composers and the growing skill of instrument makers, new, more efficient, and finer means of musical production were being fashioned.

From out of the long succession of stringed instruments two main families were evolved, the viols and the violins, which, like monkey and man, were related only by a common ancestry. Both reached a definitive stage during the sixteenth century, the viols approaching their final form earlier than their rivals. For a considerable period, they held almost undisputed sway, and a consort of viols was the most common feature of musical life. Later, the broken consort, that is, a collection of instruments of various families, was introduced, and while forming the first approach to the modern orchestra spelled the downfall of the viol. It was here that the limitations of the viols began to be discovered, and although for a time they shared the stage with the violin family, they were inevitably superseded. Their complicated mechanism and technique, and their lack of strength and penetration which was largely due to the method of holding the bow over the hand, made them unable to compete with the effective simplicity of their rivals. Thus they ceased to play any practical part in the orchestral scheme, and disappeared from its history.

It is to the Italian town of Cremona that we owe the first signs of stability in the orchestra, for it was here that the violin family, the strings of the modern orchestra, reached perfection. This is a big word to use, but since, after 250 years, mankind has not been able to discover a single improvement, apart from superficial fittings, we may assume that these instruments did, towards the end of the seventeenth century, reach the highest possible point in their development. But let us not imagine that they were then immortalized. Who knows, with the decay of taste and social feelings, these wonderful creations may be superseded by the sphereophone, the trantonium or some other future instrument of torture, and the violin, with its short and breathtaking history, may be placed on the museum-shelf beside its unadaptable predecessors.

The other instruments progressed more slowly. This is not surprising, for, whereas the violin family relied alone on the ancient craft of the wood-carver, oboes, flutes, clarinets, bassoons, trumpets, and horns called for an exactitude in metal-working, wood-turning, and a mechanical ingenuity which did not belong to the early centuries. The tone and the intonation of the precursors of these modern instruments would be execrable to our ears; even to-day when mechanical precision has reached a stage which, to a clumsy man like myself, is incredible, it is rare enough to find a wind instrument of any description which is in tune with itself right through the register. (Perhaps, if a string player were to find his way into the instrument factory, an instrument approaching more nearly to perfection might be built, but, as far as we can see, the impossibility of producing a perfectly-tuned succession of notes throughout the entire compass of any instrument based on the bore of a tube will never be overcome. But a serious study of a stringed instrument would train the ear of the player concerned, so that he might make those minute adjustments without which even good intonation cannot be obtained.)

However that may be, it was not until the first half of the eighteenth century was passed, and Haydn was writing his first symphonies, that the nucleus of the modern orchestra can be said to have been established. And then it consisted, cautiously enough, of strings, with pairs of flutes, oboes, bassoons, horns, trumpets, and a timpani or kettledrum. So much that we look for to-day had not yet justified its claim to inclusion, but at last a stable balance of strings, wood-wind, and brass had been found. As Julius Harrison, in his excellent chapters on 'The Orchestra and Orchestral Music' in *The Musical Companion*, expresses it:

The golden age of instrumental composition had arrived simultaneously with the first orchestra worthy of the name. But this was no mere chance. Melody, harmony, the making of instruments, the growth of learning and of general culture, all had progressed side by side until, midway through the eighteenth century, the long-desired end had come in sight. The future now held a promise of greatness the full measure of which no man could foresee.

The remaining instruments crept in slowly; it was, for example, not until Beethoven composed his Fifth Symphony – *the* Fifth Symphony – that the three trombones which we now take as a matter of course were first introduced into a symphony. Even then, one of the three instruments was the alto trombone, now almost obsolete. Its inherent deficiencies made it unable to maintain its place beside the tenor and bass trombones and it disappeared from regular use soon after its introduction into the symphony orchestra. The part which Beethoven wrote for it is now almost invariably played by the first tenor trombone. If we ignore the use of trombones which Purcell and Mozart had already made in their operas, the active life of these instruments from the orchestral point of view does not, therefore, exceed 140 years, although as 'sackbuts' their history can be traced back almost indefinitely. At the period under consideration, the possibilities of the various new instruments had hardly been suspected, certainly not explored. The orchestra had to wait to realize the vast dreams of Berlioz, and although in the time of Beethoven the essentials of the modern orchestra were fixed, it was not until Rimsky-Korsakov, Wagner, and Strauss had made exhaustive demands by their complicated scores that orchestral technique arrived at its peak. Of the orchestra of the future nothing can be said. There has been, indeed, a tendency among recent composers to go back to simplicity, to aim at delicate personal effects, and while this may be but a swing of the pendulum, it is hard to imagine how the orchestra can be further developed in size, weight, and technique without crossing the boundary line between music and noise.

There is the lesson of the sound film, the wireless, and, now, television to warn us of the 'shape of things to come', and although in each instance the orchestra has not been superseded, possibilities are opened up which may, unless we value our musical heritage, put an end to the long evolution from the primitive collection of instruments to the modern orchestra.

(b) *The Orchestra Emerges*

ONCE a stable basis for the orchestra had been laid, and composers had written works for a fixed combination of instruments which was capable of enlargement without any change in its nature, the question of orchestral technique became urgent. Each section of the orchestra had to develop a homogeneity and a common skill capable of merging into the general ensemble of the larger body. Along these lines, rapid development was being exacted by the demands of composers. At the same time, the taste for orchestral music was growing steadily. In Germany, where each little state had its appropriate princeling who found it necessary, whether he was musical or not, to maintain his private band, the matter was not pressing; those who frequented the courts could hear what music there was, and did not feel called upon to spread the privilege abroad.

In those countries where a unified form of government was in power, and where rapid industrialization had built up a new semi-leisured class anxious to justify itself by a wider desire for cultural activities, enthusiasts for music had to turn their attention elsewhere and create for themselves the conditions which were taken for granted in the still feudal countries. It is, therefore, not surprising that the development of permanent societies for the promulgation of orchestral music began in Great Britain and, later, in the United States of America.

When, in 1813, the Philharmonic Society of London was formed, music in this country had ceased to have much vitality since the death of Handel in 1759, and of Arne in 1778. No regular series of concerts existed, and the few that were given could hardly be called public concerts, presented as they were for the delectation of the nobility, and reaching only a very low standard. Not that the Philharmonic Society aimed – or aims to-day – at the popularization of orchestral music; it set out in the first instance to rekindle a taste for music, and to establish a professional standard of performance which would do justice to the greatness of the works presented. Considerable care was devoted to the selection of soloists, who were brought from all over the world to offer to a cultured public a reliable and authentic interpretation of the music performed. That these aims were crowned with a uniform success is proved by the history of the Society, and we should be asking too much for the creation of conditions which are only possible – and yet not realized – to-day.

A proud claim of the Society is its connexion with Beethoven, and the help and encouragement which, as the leader of British music, it extended to the great composer whose bust is now exhibited in front of the orchestral dais on the occasion of the Society's concerts. To have recognized the worth of Beethoven during his lifetime, and in a foreign country, too, was no small achievement, and a tradition of Great Britain as a patron of leading continental musicians was set up and played an important part in our native history of music. For a long period, the Society's gold medal has each year been presented to an outstanding figure in the world of music, and, not infrequently, the award has gone abroad. One wonders what might have been the effect had well-wishers for music in England pondered over the saying, 'Charity begins at home'. At the same time, it must be remembered that the cult of foreign musicians in England was not entirely due to snobbishness, although it frequently degenerated into no more than reverence for an unpronounceable name; foreign artists owed much of their popularity to a recognition and appreciation of the tradition which they represented, and from which we were able to profit, if only at second hand.

The Philharmonic Society of London missed an historic opportunity when it failed to establish an orchestra of its own at the time of its foundation. The fact that the Society had no precedent for its activities, and that it arose from a mediocre background, as I have indicated above, gives great credit to the original promoters, but the tradition subsequently built up on these foundations was limited to a dangerous extent. Although every effort was made to develop and maintain a high standard of performance, the emphasis was laid rather on the choice of music for each individual concert than on the medium for these perform-ances, soloists always excepted. Had an orchestral organiza-tion been formed early in the nineteenth century, its influence on subsequent events, quite apart from the glory it would have gained in its own right, cannot well be exaggerated. The deplorable and variable standard of playing in this country up to the twentieth century could not have satisfied listeners, any more than it would to-day, for the public would have become orchestra-conscious to a degree which is not yet reached in Great Britain.

During a concert tour of Germany which the L.P.O. made in 1936, the most striking impression I received – and this in spite of Nazi efforts, speeches, receptions, salutings, and the presence of Hitler – was the general acceptance of an orchestral musician as an artist. At the Gewandhaus, for example, one could not fail to be impressed by the fore-thought which the designers had displayed for the comfort of the musicians. Here, the bandrooms were not hidden in the most inaccessible, cold, and dirty depths of the building, as if to separate the players from the distinguished members of the public. Coming from the even more historic Royal Opera House, Covent Garden, where accommodation for the musicians of the orchestra was practically non-existent, and where backstage conditions would have horrified those who graced the *foyer* during the intervals of an extravagantly-presented opera or ballet, we could not fail to be affected by the striking contrast. A traditional respect for the artist could be felt as one entered the Gewandhaus. It was not necessary to be reminded of the glory that had gone before; dignity was in the very space and breadth enjoyed by generations of orchestral artists. And this respect was noticeable, not only among middle-class concert-goers, but with ordinary folk who, in England, were willing to accept the word of a by no means teetotal journalist who assured his readers that the members of a symphony orchestra were interested in the music they were playing only to the extent of hoping the concert would finish early enough to permit a visit to the local hostelry before closing time.

The Vienna Philharmonic and the New York Philharmonic, founded almost simultaneously some years later, were able to avoid the mistake of the London Society, although for different reasons. In Vienna, the founders of the society were fortunate in having a traditional tree from which they could branch, and in its early days the Philharmonic Orchestra was no more than an offshoot from the State Opera, giving a series of symphony concerts which enabled both the musicians and their hearers to become familiar with the great works being written. The activities of the Vienna Philharmonic have been somewhat restricted by the players' membership of and responsibility to the State Opera; when a player is absent from the latter body he must supply and pay for his deputy, and the free movement of the Orchestra has therefore been hampered. Concerts could only be given when there were no opera rehearsals or performances, and it may have been this fact which has made eleven-thirty on Sunday mornings the traditional concert time.

Although the Philharmonic Society of London can claim

the distinction of having commissioned the Ninth Symphony of Beethoven, it is the Vienna Philharmonic which is proud of having given the first performance, asserting, as Heinrich von Kralik does in his monograph on the Orchestra, that Nicolai and the Vienna Philharmonic concerts can claim to have exerted the first influence towards a true knowledge of the Choral Symphony. Some twenty years after its inception, the Orchestra became an independent, self-governing body, an artistic republic which, through periods of peace, war, starvation, and plenty, has been able to maintain its existence and integrity. A regular cycle of eight concerts is given each season, with a ninth, called the 'Nicolai concert' after its founder, of which the proceeds are devoted to the orchestral pension fund.

The New York Philharmonic also began as a democratic organization, and is even referred to by its historian, Henry Edward Krehbiel, as a 'democratic, or rather communistic, body.' This may be something of an exaggeration, for no organization can out-distance to any considerable extent the society in which it exists, and survive; but it is true that it is composed of professional musicians and has a constitution designed to prevent abuses of power. On the other hand it allows, in addition to Actual (playing) Members, a number of elected Honorary and Honorary Associate Members who are either 'eminent artists in music' or 'meritorious individuals not belonging to the profession'; and of the thirteen officers elected to direct the affairs of the Society, the two most important – the President and the Secretary – may be drawn from these categories. In 1928, the Orchestra was amalgamated with the New York Symphony Orchestra and was henceforth known as the New York Philharmonic-Symphony Orchestra.

A couple of years before the formation of the two orchestras mentioned above, the Liverpool Philharmonic Society was founded, but it followed more nearly upon the tradition of its ancestor in London. Indeed, its organization was even more exclusive, and its activities were designed for the delight of the restricted circle of members of the Society. The private nature of the Society was such that, if a member was unable to attend a concert for which he held a ticket, he could dispose of it only by offering it for sale to someone whose name appeared upon an authorized list. There was thus no danger of a member's introducing his butler or valet to the privilege and pleasure of enjoying a concert of symphonic music. It is said that when, many years later, the Society was in low water and appealed for help to the Liverpool Council, the latter body pertinently asked to be informed of the services which the Society had rendered to music during its long existence. This rebuke, which might have been shared by other similar bodies, was not unmerited and cannot be fully answered by referring back to the original aims of the founders who, acting logically for their epoch, could not be expected to legislate effectively for conditions a century hence. As in London, the importance of the concerts themselves was placed higher than that of organizing the orchestra, although the two objects can never be entirely separated. The Society has to its credit a Philharmonic Hall, a highly satisfactory building and a tangible proof of its power to survive which may well be a pride to its owners. The more so, since with the destruction by fire of its predecessor the directors of the Society might have been tempted to realize the worth of the valuable site on which it stood.

However much the future of orchestral playing may rest in the hands of the musicians themselves to-day, the progress which was made during the nineteenth and early twentieth centuries was to a large extent due to strong musical personalities, whose determination and influence made and still make themselves felt. Of these, the greatest was Sir Charles Hallé, by whose efforts Manchester became a lead-

ing city of music in Great Britain. The formation of the
Hallé Society in 1857 carried on an older tradition, but
revitalized it and directed it upon original and ambitious
lines. In its performances of new works under Hans Richter
and later conductors, in its bold style of playing, the Hallé
Orchestra built up a reputation and a reserve of orchestral
players which have taken a large part in the development of
orchestral playing throughout England. The London
orchestras which were to come later owed much to the
musicians of the North, for the Hallé Orchestra avoided the
common mistake of looking elsewhere for the talent it
needed, but found the greater part of it in its own city. The
establishment of the Royal Manchester College of Music in
1893 by Sir Charles Hallé supplied excellent training for
this native talent, and by the introduction of international
professors like Adolf Brodsky and Willy Hess profited from
the older established continental tradition. The importance
of the connexion between the Orchestra and the Manchester
College of Music cannot be over-estimated, and should have
proved a valuable example for other teaching institutions
which, if followed, would have had a far-reaching effect on
the history of orchestral music in this country. Even in
such a short note on the Hallé Orchestra mention must be
made of the late Sir Hamilton Harty. In his work for the
Orchestra he fully understood the meaning of the tradition
he was carrying on, and devoted a great deal of time and
energy to the establishment of a definite orchestral style.
That his influence was not merely local is proved by the
presence in London of many players trained by him. Leslie
Heward, whose untimely death robbed us of one of our most
promising conductors, maintained for a number of years the
traditions to which he succeeded when he followed Harty.

The Berlin Philharmonic Orchestra began its career as a
purely concert orchestra, and was a self-governing body of
players. It derived the bulk of its income from the famous

series of Philharmonic concerts, and from the general rehearsals which preceded them. For a time, its affairs were handled by a firm of concert directors; the results of this arrangement were not always to the benefit of the Orchestra. As the Berlin Philharmonic progressed it became clear that some sort of subsidy would have to be provided, and after the first world war the city of Berlin, the State of Prussia, and the German Government, the latter directly interested in the cultural value of its greatest concert orchestra, joined together to guarantee the orchestral budget up to a certain fixed limit. As one result, these bodies were represented on the board of directors of the Orchestra, a proceeding fraught with danger. Under the Weimar Republic, however, the method worked well, as the city of Berlin, insistent that no private enterprise should profit from the work of the Orchestra, saw to it that the players received more and more of their full share of the income. At this time, the Berlin Philharmonic had its own private pension fund, to which every member contributed. This fund profited from an annual concert to which the conductor gave his services.

A year after the accession of the Nazi Government to power, the whole Orchestra was taken over by the Ministry of Propaganda, and the members became Government employees with contracts and guaranteed pensions. Thus, the privileges and responsibilities, the scope and the enthusiasms were exchanged, in many cases unwillingly, for the security of servility. I well remember, at a reception given by that Orchestra to the L.P.O. at the Philharmonie in Berlin in 1936, a conversation I had with one of the violinists of the Berlin Philharmonic. He had been recounting to me, in a curiously colourless tone of voice, the many material benefits gained by the players since Hitler's coming to power. A little maliciously, perhaps, I enquired, 'Well, and are you happy now?' He gave a hurried glance around and said, with all the earnestness he could command,

'I would give everything: pensions, fees, official status, everything, for some of the freedom we used to have!'

Since the end of World War II, the Berlin Philharmonic has reverted to its old method of management, although its subsidies are uncertain, and the authorities of the American Zone of Berlin, in which its offices are situated, put considerable power into the hands of one of the conductors appointed. But the players are themselves finally responsible for solving the many problems created by the post-war situation, increased by the loss of the Philharmonie. My pre-war interlocutor had miraculously survived, a haggard but cheerful ghost of former days, to illustrate in his person the general deterioration of German musical values. It has still to be seen whether the members of this Orchestra will show the resilience which has enabled their colleagues in Vienna to surmount the aftermath of wars and revolutions.

(c) Recent History

ONE of the strongest generating forces in the history of the symphony orchestra in Great Britain has been the deputy system. Whether the system was regarded favourably or otherwise depended on the point of view of the person concerned. A conductor would go to rehearsal expecting to find certain recognized players, and be confronted with a number of strange faces or, worse still, with some that were for unpleasant reasons even too familiar to him. In his view, nothing could be more pernicious than this arrangement, hallowed though it might be by tradition, which allowed a player to send a deputy when he preferred to be playing elsewhere. But to the harassed orchestral musician it was no more than the obvious solution. A member of one of the most uncertain and insecure professions of all, he might be forced to sacrifice a permanent though less glorious position in order to fulfil this single engagement or short season.

It is true that this freedom of the player, when pushed to its ultimate limit, produced ludicrous situations, as when the man who attended the rehearsal, sitting and listening to the conductor's recommendations for three hours until certain desired effects had been obtained, was replaced on the evening of the concert by the original player who had spent the morning more profitably elsewhere. But there was some excuse for the orchestral musician, who was forced by circumstances to build a pattern from the jig-saw of his diary. No symphony orchestra at that time could offer him a living income for twelve months of the year, and the long intervening periods had to be filled in with teaching, theatres, small orchestras, and other forms of entertainment. Most of these engagements demanded a certain continuity, and overlapped inevitably with the occasional symphony concerts for which, in any case, the players were not highly paid.

Consequently, the musicians of the orchestra could not afford to take more than a short and practical view of the situation and, although they were undoubtedly aware of the anomalies of the reigning system, did not consider it their duty to correct them. They might even have argued with a certain show of justice that, if they were not allowed to send deputies, the conductor had no more right to move about as he pleased, and be frequently replaced by a much less brilliant light.

The dilemma was courageously dealt with, but not permanently solved, by Sir Henry Wood. It must be said of him that his unfailing regularity and dependability disposed of any suggestion that he employed comparable methods. After considerable experience of the shortcomings of the deputy system he put his foot down firmly, insisting on a rule that all members of the Queen's Hall Orchestra should attend regularly or not at all. For this action we owe Sir Henry a double debt of gratitude; first of all for having drawn attention to a tradition which was hampering the progress of orchestral playing, and, secondly, for having indirectly fathered a great orchestra. For a strong section of the players decided no less firmly to adhere to the old tradition and when Sir Henry maintained his stand the group of independents formed the London Symphony Orchestra – but the flaw remained. In the Queen's Hall Orchestra conditions were steadily improved to make the exacting engagement justify its sole claim on the players, but many of the best and most experienced musicians had already been lost. (By a full turn of the circle, Sir Henry in later days became a frequent conductor of the L.S.O.; time had healed the breach.)

The right to send deputies when other work proved more attractive still acted as a dragging force upon the London Symphony Orchestra, and it may be said that the most brilliant years of this organization were the three spent under a special contract which, while making exclusive demands on the players, offered adequate compensation.

Here lay the actual solution: the establishment of a truly permanent orchestra. The British Broadcasting Corporation was the first body with the financial strength to build such an organization, insisting as it did from the foundation of the B.B.C. Symphony Orchestra on the exclusive services of its members. But the B.B.C. was always an organization apart, and the establishment of its orchestra did not solve the professional problem, although it pointed the path which had to be followed. Sir Thomas Beecham had for some time worked with the L.S.O., and recognized the limitations imposed by tradition. He set his heart on building a permanent orchestra of his own, so controlled that the faults of the deputy system, and the glorious independence which went with it, would no longer exist. To this end he called a conclave of his wealthy, cultured friends, who guaranteed the losses which the orchestra must inevitably involve in spite of the many engagements which were obtained from the various societies whom Sir Thomas had persuaded to co-operate in the scheme.

The artistic success of the Orchestra, for the most part chosen from young players, is a matter of musical history, and may be regarded as the climax of Sir Thomas's career and of the continuous efforts he had made to bring British orchestral playing up to an international standard. At this period, the name of the London Philharmonic Orchestra was synonymous with that of Sir Thomas Beecham, and from the artistic point of view nothing more favourable could have been desired; but Sir Thomas, in his quality of idealist, had but little regard for the more mundane aspects of the musical scene. Fighting a valiant battle against the solid philistinism of certain sections of the British public, he never hesitated to go to extreme lengths to challenge the dead weight of cultural apathy. But the reconciliation between art and commerce, which is at any time an endless source of difficulties, meant little to the anarchic temperament of this dynamic conductor. Although always seeking the use of public and private money when his own was exhausted, he was unwilling to admit, and even unable to realize, that financial exigencies should exercise any control over the musical activities which he considered essential. Thus the inevitable happened. Many of his wealthy friends, their feet nearer the earth, became impatient with the splendid gestures which consumed their generosity, and even before the outbreak of war in 1939, the Orchestra received less and less support of that description. Only by means of an almost uninterrupted round of engagements which barely failed to play the musicians to death was it possible to balance the budget of the L.P.O.

Early in 1939, as that year slid uneasily down the descent to Avernus, it became clear that only a miracle would re-establish the financial stability of the Orchestra. It was not a period of miracles, and the last season of Grand Opera at

Covent Garden, insisted upon by Sir Thomas as a final flourish in the face of disaster, proved to be the *coup de grâce*. A few months later, the brilliant career of the L.P.O., for seven years the white-headed boy of London society, came to an ignominious end.

*

The London Symphony Orchestra, in dissociating itself from one particular conductor, and in insisting upon its right to decide its own domestic problems, played an important and even revolutionary part in the historic development of the symphony orchestra in England. The authority of the conductor as an organizer and administrator was seriously challenged for the first time.

In September 1939, when the collapse of the L.P.O. was more than imminent, it was obvious that the lines laid down thirty-five years earlier by the L.S.O. would have to be followed to a considerable degree if the Orchestra was to survive. At a doleful meeting of the creditors of the governing company, at which Sir Thomas distinguished himself in silencing and dumbfounding the most critical guests with his rhetorical eloquence, no plans for the future came to light beyond the suggestion of forming an internal committee instructed to find whether, under the conditions prevailing, the Orchestra could be kept in being.

The formation of a committee was no new thing. As a result of previous dissatisfactions committees had been elected on numerous occasions; but without status or powers they proved to be little more than another executive organ of the particular management concerned. And the more strong-minded and persistent members of these committees frequently discovered that at the end of the current season their services were no longer required. The 1939 committee decided at once that power was essential if anything constructive was to be achieved, and a new company was formed which was to admit as shareholders only playing members of the Orchestra, while all other interests were rigidly excluded. Sir Thomas, who was present at the election of the committee, approved its first actions, but, since history is a complete statement rather than an artistic selection of the facts, it must be recorded that he awoke one fine morning to regret the gift he had made to the players of all that the words 'London Philharmonic Orchestra' signified. In an historic document of four pages, typewritten copies of which were circulated to each member of the Orchestra although ostensibly addressed to the committee, Sir Thomas expounded his opinion of the democratic principle as typified by the said committee. This he did in that language of which he is past-master, and had events run true to tradition, the constitution of the L.P.O. might have suffered a sudden change. The members of the Orchestra had, however, already gained a certain faith in their elected representatives, and decided to allow the famous epistle to 'lie on the table'.

Sir Thomas's immediate reactions are not recorded, but whatever antagonism there may have been proved fortunately to be no more than a passing humour, and one which had, in any case, to be anticipated. For a time, Sir Thomas realized how much happier was the situation in which he could be first, second, and last, the conductor, unworried by the petty, frustrating details of management. This did not preclude him from proffering brilliant schemes and shrewd advice on plans and personalities, the result of a lifetime spent in fighting and evading the difficulties involved in promoting musical enterprises in England, the land without music. It was thus that we were able to enjoy two of our happiest seasons with him in 1945 and 1946, but our disinclination to accept all his advice and all his proposals drove him back to his own personal history, in which, like the Bourbons, he had 'learned nothing and forgotten nothing.' His formation of a Royal Philharmonic

Orchestra, in curious collaboration with the famous Society, is a chapter of musical history of which a full account has yet to be written. Other conductors were even more intransigent, and openly resented the newly acquired powers of the orchestral committee. This was rather naïvely expressed by one of them: 'Of course, no one will doubt that you may be a fine viola player (only I doubted it!), and that the others are excellent musicians, but people won't be very ready to entrust you with money and the management of the Orchestra.'

The early war-time days of the committee were not without their amusing aspect, although the amusement is mainly retrospective. Shut out of the Royal Opera House, Covent Garden, as the result of a change of business interests, the members of the committee, which included star performers from the Orchestra, held their daily meetings under strange conditions. Important points of procedure were decided in the rain on the pavement of Covent Garden; concerts were planned in the Spartan comforts of a Lyons' teashop; the choice of personnel was made with the assistance of more potent refreshment when the business of the day had dragged on long into the blackout. Or a sudden call from a conductor would change the décor to the lounge at Claridge's, without changing the fact that the new administration of the Orchestra had no funds and no home.

The help of a few friends and the encouragement of several desperate concerts helped to give stability and a headquarters. From that moment, the L.P.O. not merely survived; it decided to turn its attention to some of the problems which had not only worried orchestral managements, but which were holding back the development of symphonic music in England.

It was at once obvious that the good work must begin within the Orchestra. Having freed itself from subservience to one particular man or management, it had to realize the responsibilities of its newly-won privileges. It could not run the risk of handing itself over blindly to the tender mercies of a committee, whose methods might soon become no less dictatorial than those of previous bodies, unless vigilance were exerted. Every action of the new management had to be open to criticism, and although the committee might have full liberty of action during the period between annual elections, members of the Orchestra must at any time have the power to wipe clean the board of directors.

When J. B. Priestley was once explaining to a Yorkshire audience the manner in which the L.P.O. was organized, he ended by saying, 'So you see, this Orchestra is run like a soviet – if you don't mind the word!' The members of the L.P.O. were not seriously concerned with the word, but were forced by desperate circumstances to evolve a method of affairs which would keep them together for the present and enable them to build a secure foundation for the future. They agreed upon the democratic principle because it was one which adapted itself to twentieth-century conditions.

In her study of Sir Thomas Beecham in *Beecham and Pharaoh*, Ethel Smyth recounts that conductor's disagreements with various orchestral bodies, and justifies his attitude with the following remarks:

The British National Opera Company . . . kept their flag flying with varying fortunes, and were finally slain by two deadly agents The first was the Entertainment Tax. The second was, in Beecham's opinion, their adherence to the same principle which in 1932 was to cause the divorce between him and the L.S.O.; the principle of forming their business committees from the body of the artists themselves. How anyone but a baby in arms can fail to see that this principle is bound to result in a steady progression to the lowest depths of inefficiency, I do not understand.

This categorical statement, revealing a nineteenth-century prejudice which is discredited if not dead, has been proved untrue on the basis of many years' experience. The risk of proving the prejudice true is always present, for musicians, like members of most professions, are liable to put their immediate interests before those which are wider and more difficult of attainment. But such weaknesses are not peculiar to democratic organizations; on the contrary, a survey of British orchestras to-day might suggest the reverse. The compelling power of tradition is certain to be stronger in a self-governing artistic body, with its continuity of policy and its permanent self-criticism, than when the word of one person alone is law, a law subject to the many moods of a single personality, unchecked by the collective opinions of his colleagues.

After what was, in effect, a local revolution, it was not surprising to find some musicians proving themselves irreconcilable to the new régime; not from any positive dislike or disapproval of the changed system, but owing to a psychology born and matured during the pre-war era, which prevented them from approaching the new problems from any but a stereotyped angle. Every fresh development, accepted by the majority with adventurous enthusiasm, was looked upon by these few with the suspicion due to lack of understanding. But the number of these malcontents is few, and time will win over or efface their silent disapproval.

The development of such a democratic organization is a continuous process, and the results cannot be judged immediately. The committee can influence the conduct and opinions of the musicians it represents, and in its turn will react to the influence of the players themselves, while both are vitally affected by external circumstances which may control or be controlled. Although set principles are necessary in the solution of any problem, it is no less important to be ready and capable of making any change of direction demanded by a corresponding change in governing circumstances. Only thus is continued progress possible, and the continuity is visualized not merely for the lifetime of its originators, or for any specified period following it, but for good. Having struggled its way to a form which, while it fits to-day's conditions, can be readily adapted to the changes of to-morrow, the players are determined to avoid the common mistake of allowing their present or future welfare to be dependent upon any single individual. A form of organization must be found which will have in itself the life and vigour necessary for its forward movement. Individuals may make valuable contributions to its momentum, but their disappearance must not mean bankruptcy or despair. The show must go on!

2   *Conductorless Orchestras*

WHEN the members of the London Symphony Orchestra in 1904, or those of the London Philharmonic in 1939, took over the reins of self-government, they might have been excused some drastic behaviour towards conductors. After many a tedious morning with tiresome and irritating conductors an orchestral player has wearily expressed the wish that the race of this species had never begun. How wonderful it would be if an orchestra could play on its own, without the often unnecessary attentions of the 'man on the box', whose frantic gesticulations frequently conveyed little beyond the fact that he had lost his place in the score! How the musicians would display to amazed audiences that it was they, and not the wielder of the baton, who really took on the artistic responsibility of the performance! They would instance performances of such works as the *Scherzo* from Mendelssohn's *Midsummer Night's Dream* music, where, after the first bar, the conductor had folded his arms – perhaps for a rest – leaving the orchestra to rely alone on its own impetus and sense of rhythm. Then, becoming more serious, they would ask whether it would be possible to dispense with the conductor; and it would be these discussions, and the conclusions drawn from them, which dissuaded the players later from pushing their revolution to such lengths. But not without regret!

Had the players of the L.P.O. followed the less well-advised course, their action would not have been without precedent, for after the 1917 Revolution, an orchestra in Moscow did function for nearly twelve years without the stimulus of a conductor. In an article which he published in the *Radio Times* some years ago, H. N. Brailsford reminded us of the Moscow experiment when, in the absence of a conductor, a symphony orchestra decided to carry on without one. This experiment was full of interest, but although Mr Brailsford found no elements in it which are not feasible, I think anyone with orchestral experience will agree that such an experiment was destined to fail.

This opinion may seem to be negatived by the length of time for which the orchestra in question continued along these lines, but we must ask ourselves what would be the changes such an organization would have to undergo and what limitation it would have to suffer as a condition of survival.

In his article Mr Brailsford himself made some dangerous admissions. He spoke of the first trumpeter who 'by his intelligence and creative instinct had won a deserved ascendancy over his fellows', and stated that it was the same musician who, during an interval, was empowered to make certain important announcements to the audience. He said later, speaking of a performance he had heard, that 'one missed the sense that a single creative mind . . . had fused them into a single instrument to render his thought!'

If these two remarks are pitted one against the other, it will be seen that either the man of 'intelligence and creative instinct' will assume such an ascendancy over his fellows that many of the conductor's most important duties will devolve upon him, or we shall continue to miss the evidence of a single creative mind behind the performance.

In any company of men, dealing with no matter what subject, one will certainly stand out by reason of clearer insight and innate powers of leadership. Even when we are all given equal opportunities of education and development, these differences between the stature of men will continue to exist, though perhaps in a lesser degree. And since this is true, the leader will emerge and guide his fellow artists, whether it be nominally as a conductor, or tacitly as adviser and co-ordinator of the artistic ideals of others.

As proof of this, we might begin by considering the string quartet; the finest, if almost the smallest, form of concerted music. It is safe to say that, even in the best quartet, the ultimate unity of conception, style, and execution must depend on one member. All four may be fine musicians, but they will inevitably tend to express themselves in their own personal way, and this cannot make for unity of style and expression. One among them must implement and co-ordinate the various artistic outlooks, and the final unity will depend on how much ahead of the others is the co-ordinating mind. That is why one would never expect a first-rate string quartet from the four premier soloists in the world; the measure of their inability to subordinate their personalities would be the measure of their lack of unity.

In a symphony orchestra the difficulty is intensified, for not only have you a far larger variety of instruments, playing from a far more complex score, but there are groups of musicians all playing from the same part. This means that all must accept an extra-imposed idea of conception and execution. There must be, in the first place, a principal to each group whose word is law; although if he be a good principal he will fashion his word with respect to the artists behind him. Then there must be someone to sum up the conclusions of these principals and of the solo artists (wood-wind, brass, etc.) and a conductor is therefore indispensable.

The question must be considered only from a practical point of view. Undoubtedly, the average orchestral player, suffering under the lash of some crotchety or over-tempera-mental conductor, may wish the whole fraternity to the nethermost regions; but that does not solve the problem. That a conductorless orchestra can at least function is proved by the Moscow experiment, and we should be grateful to these courageous musicians for having shown us at one and the same time the limits of self-government in an orchestra, and the extent to which a conductor may be dispensed with.

The limitations should be studied. In the first place, rehearsals could only proceed by trial and error. Whereas a capable conductor will know before commencing rehearsal exactly what are the composer's intentions, what feelings and ideas he has gained from the music, and how he as conductor proposes to put them into effect, the members of an orchestra will be at first largely concerned with technical difficulties and points of ensemble which must be overcome before there can be any question of unity of ideas. Having got so far, there would have to be almost interminable discussions on the finer details of *tempo*, *nuance*, and *rubato*, which even in chamber music can absorb much time, but which in an orchestra of a hundred players might well continue indefinitely. That these discussions would be fascinating, and that those taking part would eventually become far better musicians than the members of a more normal organization, is undoubtedly true, but concerts have to be given on definite dates, and no amount of mere discussion will be sufficient to prepare a work for public performance.

The repertoire would therefore be cut down very considerably, and this would be a great loss to the public and to composers, who already find it sufficiently difficult to introduce their works. The ratio between rehearsal and performing time would be completely upset, and in our backward state of society, where concerts, if not actually run for profit, have to be so organized as to reduce the losses to a minimum, the budget would also be seriously affected.

These difficulties, which may be considered sordid, would intensify the struggle between the material and artistic sides of musical performances, and would tend to make even more necessary the emergence of some artistic leadership and authority within the orchestra.

While I was enquiring into this question, I discussed the matter with several musicians who had been to Moscow. Subsequently, I went there myself. Egon Petri, who had frequently played with this conductorless orchestra, told me that the experiment had been given up for some time, and that all orchestras in the Soviet Union now had conductors. However, he confirmed many of the points I have made above; the greater number of rehearsals needed and the interminable discussions which arose with them. He told a story of the double-bass player who complained that he was unable to hear the pianist's left hand, and requested that he should play a little louder. Mr Petri added that the leader was, in effect, the conductor. This fact, savouring as it does of the days of Spohr, goes to prove the wisdom of those responsible for abandoning this interesting experiment, which threatened to prove a reversal to methods already outworn. In doing this they confirmed what we had already anticipated.

A definite leader had emerged who, though not officially conductor, did in fact train the orchestra at rehearsals. When the requisite standard of playing had been reached under his guidance the concert was given – without a conductor. It will be seen, therefore, that their experiment has solved none of the problems I have indicated above; it has, however, dealt drastically with the status of the conductor, his relations with the public and to the orchestra, and the extent of his ascendancy over his fellow artists. It is to these problems that we in England might well turn our attention.

*

The view that the experiment had failed did not seem to be held by one of those mainly responsible for carrying it through. When I met Lev Tseitlin, now an old man teaching the violin at the Moscow Conservatoire, he spoke with great regret that the work had to be given up, and gave a purely practical reason for it. The conductorless orchestra had come about, encouraged no doubt by the libertarian atmosphere of the period, when the members of two of Moscow's orchestras found themselves free from all commitments on Mondays, and decided to join forces away from the eagle eye of a conductor. He assured me that the whole thing went as smoothly as possible, and would never have ceased to exist, had not the authorities of the Bolshoi Theatre decided to call their players on Monday, thus cutting the orchestra in half. But to show his lack of animus against conductors, he told me how warm a feeling he had always maintained for Sir Henry Wood, with whom he had played many times during a stay in London half a century ago.

Other conductors also knew the orchestra. Nicolai Malko, who left Russia in 1929, was very familiar with its work, and approved highly. In his opinion, instrumental style, tone and balance did not exist in Russia until this orchestra had discovered what the terms meant and how to realize them. The players had done fundamental work in their experiment, which had influenced the whole of Soviet orchestral playing. Serge Koussevitzky did not demur from this opinion, but with his practical mind he repeated many of the objections set out earlier in this chapter, convinced that they outweighed any positive achievements.

Regretfully, I believe him to be right. The clock of progress cannot be put back, and the conductor is the natural outcome of the complexities of the modern symphony orchestra. But we can still make the best of him.

3 *The Leader of the Orchestra*

THE functions of the orchestral leader have diminished in number and importance as those fulfilled by the conductor have increased. Gone are the days when the leader's bow had a life independent of the fiddle it was designed to play upon; when the orchestra looked to him for the opening of the music, and the audience waited upon his will.

In some memoirs published in 1830, the principal oboe-player at Covent Garden tells the following story:

At the Grand Commemoration of Handel in 1784, two very pompous gentlemen, Dr Hayes of Oxford and Dr Miller of Doncaster, came to town to give their gratuitous assistance as conductors, by beating time. After several meetings and some bickerings, it was at length agreed that Hayes (Mus.D.Oxon) should conduct the first act and Dr Miller the second. With regard to the third, I suppose they were to toss up for it. When the time of performance had arrived, and Mr Cramer, the leader, had just tapt his bow (the signal for being ready) and looked round to catch the eyes of the performers, he saw, to his astonishment, a tall, gigantic figure, with an immense powdered toupée, full dressed, with a bag and sword, and a roll of parchment in his hand.

> . . . The son of Hercules he justly scorned
> By his broad shoulders and gigantic mien.

'Who is that gentleman?' said Mr Cramer. 'Dr Hayes,' was the reply. 'What is he going to do?' 'Beat time.' 'Be so kind,' said Mr Cramer, 'to tell the gentleman that when he has sat down I will begin.' The Doctor, who never anticipated such a 'set down' as this, took his seat, and Mr Cramer did begin, and His Majesty and all present bore witness to his masterly style of leading the band.

The gigantic figure with his toupée, bag, and sword is a striking prototype of many latter-day conductors, and orchestral players will chuckle delightedly at his discomfiture, but alas! Time has his revenges, and to-day the usurper has established himself in a seemingly unshakable position. How he has achieved this is not our immediate concern, which is to consider the limited power left to the leader in this occupied territory, but it is interesting to see how quickly, and how thoroughly, the change-over was made. On the concert programmes of the first seven years of the Royal Philharmonic Society two names were to be found, one described as 'Leader', and the other as 'At the Piano'. Such a division of responsibility was not calculated to continue long with any measure of success, and gradually the musician at the piano, armed as he was with the score, and called upon to make up orchestral weakness and deficiencies, assumed more importance.

In 1820, Ludwig Spohr arrived in London, and at one concert introduced a symphony of his own composition, astonishing the musical world by producing a baton and directing the orchestra with it. From that day onwards, the phrase 'At the Piano' disappeared and the term 'Conductor' took its place, although the status of the latter was yet to be defined or established. As far as the Philharmonic Society was concerned, this was achieved in no uncertain manner by Michael Costa, who, when invited to become conductor of the series in 1846, wrote to the Secretary:

I beg to acknowledge the receipt of your letter in reply to which allow me to state that the stipulations I named I consider to be no more, than would be required by any Conductor really interested in the welfare of the Philharmonic Society, and as I am firmly convinced that no Orchestra can go well unless the entire control is placed in the hands of him who is the only responsible person for the accurate performance, and if the Directors do not give me that power, I am of necessity compelled to relinquish the Engagement they offer me, but I hope upon reconsideration they will see that all I ask is necessary for the Success of the Institution.

There, without any waste of full-stops, was the knock-out blow for the leader, and, even if we to-day are inclined to disagree that the conductor is 'the only responsible person for the accurate performance', the directors at that time accepted his statement, and the writer of the letter reigned as a dictator for eight years.

It must be obvious that, in a modern symphony orchestra of from ninety to a hundred players, the term 'leader' is hallowed more by tradition than by actual usage. He is more correctly described as the principal violin, or the *violon solo*, as the French say. Nevertheless, he is still responsible for leading his own section, and through them, to a lesser extent, the rest of the strings. He will demonstrate on his instrument how certain awkward passages are to be played, and decide knotty points of fingering and bowing when called upon by wise conductors to do so. In such matters he will have the final word in any consultation which may be held between him and other string departments. But even this responsibility and privilege is in danger of being lost, for in these busy days of extensive repertoires and complicated works the leader has hardly time to spend in marking parts. Many conductors, following the example of Sir Henry Wood, make a practice of attending to these details themselves, only deferring to the leader when the intricacies of certain passages are beyond their technical knowledge.

As the solo violin of the orchestra, the leader has to-day more than ever to do. From Richard Strauss onwards, modern composers have shown a marked predilection for the particular tone quality of the solo violin against an orchestral background, and although all such solos may not present the difficulties of that in *Heldenleben*, the modern leader, with limited leisure for private practice, must be a man of resource.

He must also be a man of tact, for he is in effect the liaison officer between the orchestra and the conductor, and although a resident chief may present few problems, a guest conductor, by strange methods or lack of understanding, may disturb the equilibrium. I remember having seen a leader tell a visiting conductor very bluntly that his attitude to the orchestra was far from satisfactory and that, if he persisted in it, he alone would be to blame for a bad performance. But the same leader, on another occasion, roundly rebuked an orchestral player who, when asked to obtain a certain effect by an extremely capable conductor, insisted that it was impossible, although this was proved not to be the case. The maintenance of this balance, with the moral responsibility it involves, is no easy task, and in the performance of it the leader will soon expose his individual character. If he is the born leader, he will join a strong personality to his purely musical qualifications, gaining the admiration and confidence of his colleagues, and creating a feeling of unity in the orchestra which will react favourably upon the musical results.

A leader may take charge of sectional string rehearsals, and is not infrequently called upon to act as deputy conductor. *Habitués* of the Proms will remember how Charles Woodhouse often used to take over the second half of the concert, in the days before the adoption of these concerts by the B.B.C. Paul Beard, when leader of the London Philharmonic Orchestra, often took charge of rehearsals when Sir Thomas Beecham failed to appear and his successors have on occasions conducted the same orchestra at rehearsals and in public. The appointment (although temporary) of an assistant conductor has deprived the leader of yet another of his few remaining duties.

That this last hold of the leader is being rapidly loosened was indicated during the Promenade Seasons which have taken place since 1940. At Queen's Hall in 1940, Mr Basil Cameron was given a share of the work, and in 1941 when the season was transferred to the Royal Albert Hall, he conducted the second half of the programme at most performances. Since the death of Sir Henry Wood and with the introduction of three orchestras to the season, a further division has been made, and three conductors (with others as assistants) share the concerts between them. And the leader of the orchestra remains seated upon his own narrowed rights.

On the concert platform in England the leader does not make his appearance until the orchestra is comfortably seated and in tune – or approximately so. His delayed appearance, usually greeted with applause, is probably a relic of the leader's more glorious days, for now he is little beyond the herald of that greater personage, the conductor. In the United States, the entry of the leader has a more practical significance. Although the audience does not mark his appearance with applause, his own colleagues are made aware of it, for all preluding ceases, he takes the A from the oboe, and then satisfies himself that the remaining players are also in tune. There is a great deal to be said in favour of this practice.

During the concert the leader should, by his confident entries, give a feeling of conviction to those sitting behind him, and should be eternally on the *qui vive* for any loose rhythms and shaky ensemble-playing, so that he may correct such faults before they become perceptible to the listener. At the conclusion of the performance, especially if it has been a successful one, he will, on behalf of his colleagues, receive the thanks of the conductor, which are often publicly bestowed by one or more handshakes. Personally, I consider these exhibitions of mutual congratulation in public to be out of place, and am often tempted to look down for the recumbent figure of the particular composer who, by the united efforts of the conductor and orchestra, has so valiantly been overcome. But since music is to many an emotional recreation, one must not begrudge anything which adds to their experience.

It is an unwritten law that the members of the orchestra shall remain in their seats until the applause has died away. Only the conductor goes off, presumably in order to arouse even greater rounds of applause for his subsequent returns, which, if the concert is being broadcast, will persuade the listeners-in that they have missed an outstanding performance. This unwritten law does, however, put an unpleasant weapon into the hands of the leader, and a conductor who has been foolish enough to offend the players at rehearsal may, on returning to take the applause, have to weave his way through the ranks of the instrumentalists who, following their leader's example, are leaving the platform before the recognized moment. The audience may then continue to applaud out of sympathy, which will be poor consolation for the unfortunate conductor. While deprecating behaviour in such sorry taste, it serves to show that the leader still retains certain powers, and that the victory of the conductor is not yet complete.

4 *Conductors Face to Face*

AN old proverb among orchestral players tells us that 'the baton makes no sound', or, as José Iturbi, the brilliant Spanish pianist-conductor, once put it, 'the baton is always in C major'. These sayings illustrate the tendency among orchestral players to disparage the noble art of conducting; not because it is less important, less involved, or less difficult of achievement than any other art, but that it is the most easily exploited and, as the proverb indicates, one which makes the faults of its exponents difficult to detect.

Concert-goers often fail to realize how much of a conductor's success is due to the musicians he directs, and how much is properly due to him. The critics, one may suppose, know better, but they also frequently fail to allot praise or blame correctly, and are indeed to be forgiven for their tendency to cast the limelight on the more prominent figure of the conductor, whose name is known and the details of whose private life and public career have already provided interest for their readers. At the same time, as Ernest Newman has pointed out, the grim figure of the law of libel stands as a warning to the enterprising critic who might be tempted to express his exact opinion of the worth of this or that conductor. Until those who expose their gifts to the public eye are prepared to accept the criticism their work

54

draws upon them, critics must be content to influence their readers more by implication than by plain statement.

It is not surprising, therefore, that the ordinary listener goes to a concert with his mind already made up for him, and rarely dares to think and judge for himself, if such thinking and judging take him off the beaten track of criticism. He may hold the opinion that differences between the qualities of various conductors are so subtle that they are of no great importance; that 'a Hair perhaps divides the False and True.' A little reflection will, I am sure, reveal fundamental differences which must be appreciated if the music behind it all is to have the attention it deserves.

It is true, for instance, that many orchestral performances reach a standard of relative excellence *in spite of* the conductor. I remember how a famous conductor once brought in the orchestra (or, rather intended to do so!) during a silent bar. The moment of agony suffered by the musicians during their unanimously successful effort in resisting the conductor's command deserves an epic verse – the chord arrived in the right place one bar later. And I recall, too, another conductor who, in his exuberance at the end of Tchaikovsky's *Francesca da Rimini*, which concludes with a series of syncopated chords, beat one bar too many. Had the offender in either of these cases been, for example, a trombone player, how the critics would have pounced! And if in either case the trombone player had really relied on the conductor's indications, what sensation and amusement! But most conductors would have taken the applause unblushingly.

A story which is told of Sir Thomas Beecham throws a new light on such incidents. In his younger days Sir Thomas was to conduct a performance of *La Bohème*. The librarian, busy with the arrangement of the parts, asked the young conductor if he was familiar with the score.

'I haven't seen it yet,' was the reply.

'It might be wise to have a look at it before the rehearsal,' advised the librarian.

'Perhaps I will,' said Sir Thomas, but when he arrived at the theatre the score was still a complete stranger to him. The traditional variations of *tempo* in the operas of Puccini offer a series of traps for the unwary, and, after some time, various bars began to go astray, until at last, during a silent passage, Sir Thomas was still conducting vigorously with a special eye to the percussion.

'Why are you not playing, my dear sir?' He addressed himself to the leader of the kitchen department.

'I have nothing to do in this place,' replied the idle player.

'But, my dear fellow, it is the bounden duty of the percussion department to support me at such moments.'

The incidents I have mentioned are trifling enough, and I refer to them merely to show that even great conductors nod. But what of the mediocrities who stand proudly before orchestras which they falsely believe they are leading?

Let us, for the moment, decide what are the essential qualifications of the true conductor; we can then sift the wheat from the chaff. He needs to be a fine all-round musician, not necessarily with a great academic knowledge, for the acquisition of this may have dried up the emotions, but he must be able to sense all that is best in a musical work. He must have a highly-developed feeling for rhythm in addition to a metrical sense; the distinction is important, as the metrical perception without the rhythmical will make good phrasing an impossibility. He must have an ear so quick, accurate, and highly trained – *l'oreille fine*, in short – that the slightest error or lack of balance in the orchestral chord is instantly detected. He should be, on the rostrum at least, a man of few but effective words, capable of so indicating by his technique what effects he desires that not many verbal explanations are necessary. For this he needs the peculiar gift with the 'stick' which will have little or no relation to his qualities as a musician (many fine musicians handle the baton like a walking-stick, and some charlatans have just the right manner).

And, while we are speaking of charlatans, it must be admitted that a touch of showmanship is not to be ignored. Provided that is is no more than an effective manner of approaching the public, and does not detract from sincere musicianship, it will not adversely affect the work of the conductor. He will need, in addition, a moderate sense of humour (one must not expect too much), the patience of Job, and above all, a gift for understanding the peculiar psychology of what must, in the nature of things, be one of the most difficult bodies to handle. He need not be a disciplinarian unless he lacks this psychological knowledge of the orchestra, when the weight of his administrative powers may achieve, at best, a poor imitation of the discipline which a real sympathy will evoke.

Add the obvious, but not ever-present, qualifications of score-reading and time-beating, and it will be realized that the lack of first-rate conductors is not surprising.

One might, indeed, be tempted to ask with a certain boldness why some of our present-day conductors ever took to this branch of the art. It is too big a career to be chosen arbitrarily, and while it may be a natural development for a musician to *become* a conductor, it is a curious decision for a young man to *intend* to become a conductor. In most cases, such young men have had no experience inside the orchestra, they have little or no knowledge of the technique of the instruments which comprise the orchestra, and, last but not least, they have had no opportunity of proving or even discovering whether they possess those innate qualities of leadership which are absolutely indispensable. They may fondly imagine that a period of study at the feet of a successful conductor, and an acquaintance with a restricted number of scores, will suffice to place them in the front rank; but very few orchestral players will agree with them.

The conductor's platform is no place for the prodigy, that affliction of the musical world to which some reference must be made. We are visited from time to time by these charming infants, reputed to be nine or ten years old, who, to the delight of their more infantile parents, stand in front of an orchestra in a performance of this master-work or that. Their appearances, and the comment which they occasion, call the whole art of the conductor into question. These prodigies attract large audiences and completely upset critical balance. If they did no more it would matter little, for an uninstructed public and a few susceptible newspaper-men will always rally round on such occasions. Besides, there is in all of us some spare maternal or paternal feeling which is gratified by the sight of a wonder child. Not a bad thing, perhaps, but one which has nothing to do with music.

Until I had written the following pages I had not seen one of these boys in action. Under the emotional excitement engendered by a large crowd at a popular concert, I too might have surrendered the sober judgement needed to keep the performance in its proper perspective. For this is a matter of artistic principle, in the consideration of which a cool head and a detached attitude are essential.

Unfortunately, a number of musicians, unable to maintain any objectivity against the prevailing enthusiasm of the audiences, and accustomed to dealing with students of moderate talents, fell into the same trap with their less responsible fellow-citizens, and I was told by one of them – with no apparent qualms about the import of his statement – that an Italian prodigy was in the 'Tommy Beecham class'. This is beyond comment as a piece of self-criticism, and the remark of an orchestral player, who placed the prodigy as the best conductor of the season in which he took part, was what we used to call a 'backhanded slap' at the other worthy wielders of the baton.

Doubtless, this particular boy was extraordinarily gifted. His knowledge of the scores which enabled him to dispense with them, to sing the cues for the different instruments and to mark the parts when doubts occurred, is no mean achievement, while his stick technique seems to have made many older exponents appear clumsy and inefficient. But how far does this take us on the road to making music? There have been boys who, at an early age, could repeat the whole of *Macbeth* or even *King Lear* from memory, but I would confidently defy such a phenomenon to reveal as much of the subtle meaning of Shakespeare's profound but hidden truths as you and I know already. And it is precisely an analogous enlightenment about music that we rightly demand from a conductor.

Conducting an orchestra is at once the easiest of the executive branches of music, and the most difficult. It will remain as easy for a would-be conductor to impose on the public just as long as that public is unable to estimate his worth for itself. And to arrive at a true estimate is the most difficult thing in the world. When I played in an orchestra I could, with confidence and after a brief acquaintance, sum up the worth of conductors as they came along. Nowadays, when I meet the conductors in person, have long and varied conversations with them, and then listen with all my powers of concentration to the performances under their direction, confidence in my own judgement is far less sure, and I hasten to get as many opinions as possible from my colleagues in the orchestra before I dare to confirm my own impressions to the extent of re-engaging any particular conductor. Even so, I find many grey-haired, sober, and honest critics hopelessly misleading in their indications to the public. So let us agree that it is a difficult business.

Yet if a boy of nine or ten is in the 'Beecham class', what

is all the fuss about? Why do we reverence a Bruno Walter, a Victor de Sabata, an Eduard van Beinum, or, which is more to the point in these days of universal money valuation, why do we treat them like princes? If a boy of nine or ten can achieve it all, what are we to think of Victor de Sabata again when, after a performance which has enraptured orchestra, public, and critics, he leaves the concert hall in a state of utter dejection because for some imperceptible reason he has failed at the final moment to make the meaning of this or that phrase as clear as he himself understands it?

To learn a number of scores from memory is a great feat for a small boy, but for an adult it presents few difficulties, especially in these days of gramophone recordings which offer endless repetitions of the sound itself. Victor de Sabata can produce a hundred operas and an interminable list of symphonic works without reference to a score; but it is not this amazing power which makes him one of the greatest orchestral directors in the world. It is precisely the 'unwritten music', as it was once happily described, that we demand from a conductor. Much nonsense has been written, particularly when Toscanini's art is mentioned, about playing the music just as the composer intended it. The composer's intentions are only vaguely indicated by the marks he makes on paper; the interpretative artist is only a little less creative when he brings the music to life. The silky sheen which Bruno Walter throws over the tone of the strings, the exquisite phrasing and emotional depth plumbed by Beecham, the tense tautness, brilliance, and breathless excitement of de Sabata; these are some of the qualities which make music a vital thing, with a life beyond what the composer himself envisaged. It is just the subtle nuances, the almost imperceptible *rubati*, the personal manner of handling dynamics, which reveal the conductor. One assumes that he will be able to take the score of a work totally unknown to him, master it rapidly and create the tone-picture it represents, but his final hallmark is his leadership of the orchestra. If you are prepared to make a ten-year-old boy the captain of a ship or a major in a military unit, and then to trust your life to his guidance and direction, I am ready to entrust an orchestra and the finest music to a conductor of the same age. But not otherwise.

It may be foolish to assert that only an old man can be seriously considered as a conductor, but it is no less foolish to expect complete artistic satisfaction from the work of a young man. Among interpretative artists, the conductor needs more than any other a wide human background and an experience of life which cannot in any way be crammed into adolescence. 'One crowded hour of glorious life' never made a great conductor.

It will rarely take an orchestra more than one rehearsal to recognize the quality of a conductor. The players will not go through the list of qualifications I have stipulated above to discover where he is outstanding or deficient, but will know instinctively whether he is master of the situation and worthy of their respect. Woe betide the conductor who fails to gain it! Even without antagonism, and with the best will in the world, it is impossible for him to obtain the confidence of his fellow-artists. No royal road can be followed in obtaining the sympathy and respect of orchestral players when their collective opinion is in play. I have known conductors who treated them abominably, and have yet been admired and followed implicitly, while others who have shown consideration and kindness have failed entirely to arouse the enthusiasm or command the loyalty of any group of men. It ultimately comes down to a question of musical personality; when players are convinced that the conductor is musically sincere and is expressing music through himself rather than himself through music, they will go every inch of the way with him. The 'natural antipathy' which is said to exist between players and conductors is no more than an expression of the lack of faith in conductors who, for one reason or another, fail to impress orchestral musicians.

If conductors were to be categorically graded with any degree of accuracy, it would be impossible to put any two in the same class, but we can roughly divide them into three. First, there is the class of the truly great, that of Toscanini and Beecham, which is so restricted that it would be difficult to find four or five at any given time. These definitely add something to the sum-total of the playing of the orchestra, and obtain results which are never equalled by other conductors. They might be called the creative conductors. Then there are those who, while contributing little or nothing of their own, enable a good orchestra to do its normal best. This class is far more numerous, and orchestral music will never be in danger while they remain in charge, for their sincerity and general musicality will keep performances at a high level. Last of all, we have the largest class, a very heterogeneous one, which includes so many who have become conductors because, as Bernard Shaw might have said, 'he who can, plays, he who cannot, conducts.' Here we have the honest but dull time-beaters whose faults are at least negative, and the dishonest but brilliant charlatans who earn the hatred of musicians and the adoration of the less discerning among concert-goers.

It can be said, I think, without exaggeration, that any member of a leading symphony orchestra could take up the baton at least adequately, if not with distinction. The simple technique of conducting is fatally easy to acquire, and most orchestral players take to it quite naturally, as a result of having studied it in the practice of others. How many conductors, on the other hand, even understand the mysteries and technical difficulties of the instruments under their control, quite apart from being able to play them? Is it too much to ask that they should be sufficiently familiar with the playing technique of any instrument to avoid the exasperation caused by their ignorance? To be told in a patronizing way by the pianist-conductor that a passage for a certain instrument is 'quite easy' when the mechanics of the instrument make it well-nigh impossible, or to play from parts 'bowed' by a conductor in such a manner as to render the performance ludicrous, is no uncommon experience, but such arrogant nonsense is not calculated to facilitate co-operation between orchestra and conductor.

There is the story of the difficult clarinet solo in Rimsky-Korsakov's *Coq d'Or*. At the rehearsal the first clarinet player, who was unfamiliar with the work, slipped up rather badly. As he left the rehearsal room he passed the conductor, who gaily whistled the offending passage to him.

'There you are, Mr X; that's how it should go.'

'Oh, yes!' replied the disgruntled wind-player, 'I can whistle the damn thing.'

Edric Cundell once spoke to me of the feeling of deep respect with which he always approached the professional symphony orchestra.

'I regard an orchestra as a body,' he said, 'and I am quite over-awed by the sum of musical knowledge possessed by that body. In almost every single branch of music to which I might refer, there would be found one member, at least, whose knowledge exceeded mine.'

The reader will excuse me, as an erstwhile orchestral player, from daring to place our best-known conductors in the classes to which I think they belong; to do that would be to prevent him from beguiling the tedium of a winter's evening in this amusing pursuit. Besides, if he is persuaded to do a little field-work on his own I shall not have written in vain. He will also, I hope, exonerate me from the charge of underrating the importance of a conductor in a symphony orchestra; I have pointed out in a previous chapter that it is not possible to do without one. All I ask is that the whole

63

relationship of the conductor to the orchestra he directs should be considered from a balanced point of view. He should primarily be regarded *as a member of the orchestra*, and his contribution to the performance should be more accurately assessed. Since it is possible with an efficient orchestra for a conductor to hide his deficiencies from the public, it is important that his sincerity as an artist be proved. In his work with the orchestra he should behave as a colleague; all signs of violent 'temperament' should be avoided, for although it is true that no great conductor storms at his men, it is common for their imitators to behave in this way, while an orchestral player who gave way to such feelings would soon find himself without a job.

The public is largely at fault in this matter. By surrounding the whole business with an aura of glory and adulation it has invested the conductor's craft with an air of importance which only a truly sincere man can justify. Players are consequently subjected to the often ill-tempered attacks of men whose artistic, technical, and mental qualities are inferior to those of the rank and file of the orchestra with which they work.

It would be an excellent thing if any young man with the conductor's rostrum as the height of his ambition would follow the example given by the careers of his greatest predecessors. Richter as a horn-player, Nikisch as a violinist, Toscanini with a cello, all served their musical apprenticeship in a symphony orchestra, and the intimacy which later was to produce such splendid results was largely due to this early experience. Among younger conductors, Basil Cameron and Eugène Goossens were violinists at Queen's Hall, while Barbirolli was a distinguished cellist. This might lead us to conclude, not without justice, that no conductor should be given an important appointment until he has had twelve months' experience as an orchestral player. This would correct the grossest errors to which conductors are liable, while a more objective attitude on the part of critics and the general public would eliminate those who have no justifiable claim to such positions.

*

There is another aspect of the conductor question in England which is worth consideration, particularly as it affects our prospects for the immediate future. Conditions of musical life in this country offer little in the nature of a career to any man who feels himself fitted to become a conductor. He may have made a striking impression at the students' concerts of the institution where he has been trained, but he will be of little service to a symphony orchestra until he has had a great deal of experience, and this he will find almost impossible to obtain. Where, indeed, is he to acquire the knowledge of himself and of his subject which comes from handling large bodies of professional musicians?

If we are to assume that he must earn his living, then the way will be thoroughly obstructed. It may be true that in each generation or so one man of outstanding personality and drive may reach the front rank of symphony orchestra conductors, but he will usually bear the marks of his ascent, and will be hampered by the many years spent in activities of the wrong kind. Even so, he is no more than the fortunate exception. For the others, there may be an orchestra on the pier or in the pump-room, or in connexion with one of the provincial B.B.C. orchestras, but not one of these could properly be called a symphony orchestra, although the players composing it might be of first-rate quality. Too long a stay in such a post would distinguish the conductor with a shameful stigma, and to his dying day he would be known as Mr X, the Wytown-on-Sea conductor.

If he were still less fortunate, he would have to content his soul with a semi-amateur concern, or a choir which would be accompanied on its great days by an orchestra *d'occasion.* No ambitious conductor (and this adjective is inseparable from the substantive) would regard any such appointment as more than a stepping-stone, and it is not unusual for the United States to offer positions of more scope. If the musician honoured in this way can adapt himself to the American scene he is lost to us; Eugène Goossens and John Barbirolli are only two of our most promising young men who went the way of the 'Blue Boy'. America failed to hold either of them, and Goossens went to Australia, and Barbirolli is making musical history in Manchester. Should America prove no home from home, as in the two cases mentioned, the conductor may return to England unknown, with an American prestige which will not overcome the necessity of beginning his career all over again. When Basil Cameron came back to England in 1939 his colleagues remembered him and the high promise he had made before he went to the United States, but it was not until late in 1941 that he was established with the public, and but for the war it might have taken longer still. To this depressing list of opportunities can be added a few positions in connexion with Sadler's Wells or Covent Garden, one or two municipal appointments, and the dismal page is closed. And we wonder why the art of conducting in England languishes!

No, to become a successful conductor of symphony orchestras in England demands a careful choice of parents. Given a rich inheritance, undoubted genius, and even a secret capacity for hard work, any man can become a Sir Thomas Beecham; and a combination of the first and third attributes will often prove far more efficacious than of the second and third. Even under these most favourable conditions it will need half a lifetime before talent is recognized, and the art of publicity will have to be assiduously cultivated to persuade the public to yield what the critics deny. Only a young man driven by the urge of genius, or by the frettings of an inferiority complex, will live to overcome the difficulties and despair of such a career; and he may often wonder whether it was worth the money.

Such is the unhealthy situation which drives us to invite foreign conductors over here at a cost of public and private money which, properly expended, would go far towards developing our native talent. But if we have to wait for a war to find our own wheat crops inadequate, nothing less than a revolution will make us realize our folly where orchestral conductors are concerned.

5 Should the Composer Know Best?

IN his 'memoirs' Hector Berlioz recounts an episode from his student life which has a pointed significance to-day, more than a century later. Describing his visits to the Opera in Paris, he says:

Knowing every note of the score I would have let myself be chopped in pieces rather than let the conductor take liberties with it. Wait quietly and write my expostulations? Not exactly! No half-measures for me!

There and then I would publicly denounce the sinners and my remarks went straight home.

For instance, I noticed one day that in *Iphigenia in Tauris* cymbals had been added to the Scythian Dance, whereas Gluck had only employed strings, and in the Orestes recitative the trombones, that came in so perfectly appropriately, were left out altogether. I decided that if these barbarisms were repeated I would let them know it and I lay in wait for my cymbals.

They appeared.

I waited, although boiling over with rage, until the end of the movement, then in the moment's silence that followed I yelled:

'Who dares play tricks with Gluck and put cymbals where there are none?'

The murmuring around may be imagined. The public, not being particularly critical, could not conceive why that young idiot in the pit should get so excited over so little. But it was worse when the absence of the trombones made itself evident in the recitative. Again that fatal voice was heard:

68

'Where are those trombones? This is simply outrageous!'

I afterwards heard that the unlucky trombones were only obey-ing orders . . . After that night the proper readings were restored.

The 'young idiot' who dealt with these sins of omission and commission in so peremptory a manner gained little beyond his immediate victory; were he alive to attend concerts to-day he would not lack stimulus to rouse his ire and call forth his vehement protests.

In the episode quoted above, Berlioz mentions two specific cases, but the principles involved are of great im-portance. Has the conductor the right to add, change, or take away from the score as it was completed by the composer?

Many, if not most, conductors will answer in the affirma-tive, and will produce arguments to support their contention, but the concert-goer must decide for himself whether these arguments are sound or specious. It is often said, for example, that 'had the composer lived to-day, he would have taken advantage of certain instrumental advances, and would have rescored such and such a passage.' Since the composers in question are dead and silent, the argument is weakened by its purely conjectural nature, and is founded upon a failure to appreciate the essential unity between instru-mentation and the musical thought it is called upon to express. This applies perhaps with less force to composers of the Bach-Handel period, when the orchestra was in its infancy and was still unformed and changing, when music by its polyphonic nature relied less on the manner of its presentation than on its form. Music of this period might be called 'black and white' music, with design having a greater importance than colour. But once the modern orchestra had been established the argument lost its power. Beethoven, as he himself said, received his musical ideas as if he heard an instrument playing them, and we can safely assume that he was able to imagine mentally the sound obtained from an orchestra. And his instrumentation was undoubtedly part and parcel of his musical imagining.

When it comes to Brahms, who is in many ways a test case, and who suffers a great deal at the hands of the re-editing conductor, even the slightest justification disappears. We are told that a certain passage for orchestra is thick and muddly, and that it can be 'improved' by altered instrumentation. That it can be changed is true enough, but improved – who knows? The orchestra has not changed vitally since Brahms' day, and he was no hermit hiding from society, and avoiding performances of his own or other composers' works. He knew how his own compositions sounded in performance, had played and conducted many of them. If his judgement of orchestral balance was faulty, as it may have been, there it is; that is Brahms. In the same way, his or another's sense of melody may have been no less open to criticism, but are we to re-shape the phrases and re-mould them 'nearer to the heart's desire'?

Such attempts always remind me of the B.B.C. accent and its standard pronunciation, with the tendency to level out all individual variety and character. If the 'improving' I have spoken of were carried out logically and to its ultimate conclusion it would not be long before we should need the services of a musicologist to testify to the authorship of any music performed. Is this Debussy or Mendelssohn?

Some conductors have argued that owing to acoustical variations in different halls, certain changes in scoring are made necessary. Some parts are doubled, others lightened or redistributed to preserve a normal balance. This may sound persuasive and give the impression that the conductor concerned is one of the more sensitive and knowledgeable of his kind, but one must not be too hasty. A sketch of Toscanini, which I give in the words* of a French cellist, Robert Bergmann, himself a composer and an orchestral

*Translated – T.R.

player who had taken part in a long tour with him, throws some light on the matter:

We had a 'run-through' at a brand-new, gleaming theatre, very much the *chic* music-hall, and not designed for concerts. A concert orchestra is usually arranged in the familiar manner, the strings in front on a level, with the wood-wind and brass behind in tiers. Here it is just the reverse; the violins cascade towards the orchestra stalls, while in the rear the wind instruments are heaped up on a billiard-table surface. And, to make matters worse, there is no ceiling above the orchestra.

Toscanini examines the premises with visible distrust. He listens, and is able to hear, although we have not yet unpacked our instruments; he has an auditory sense quite incomprehensible to the uninitiated ... At the concert, with simple indications of his stick and of his magic left hand, Toscanini modifies, moulds, and apportions the quantities of sound differently; one feels that he is listening from a distance, and that, mentally, he is controlling the sound from all points of the hall. Thus the trick is done – a master trick – and the hall sounds well. But Toscanini, the alchemist of sound, has had to work harder than on other occasions.

The personal taste of conductors is not the sole cause of incomplete orchestration of the kind which infuriated Berlioz. Concert promoters with lack of foresight often include one item in a programme which calls for an instrument not otherwise required for the performance. Upon discovering this they may decide that its inclusion is 'not very important', that the notes it should play are doubled by another instrument and that its services need not be engaged. Conscientious conductors will have none of this cheeseparing, and there is an account of Sir Henry Wood which illustrates an attitude of respect for the composer's work. I cannot vouch for the truth of the story, but it is so much in character that it will bear repetition here.

Sir Henry was engaged to conduct a programme in a provincial town, and upon arrival at rehearsal on the day before the concert discovered to his disquiet that no contrabassoon had been engaged, although the score of one work contained an important phrase for that instrument.

'I refuse to spoil the ship for a ha'porth of tar,' he said, and insisted that a telegram be sent to a player in London to attend for the concert. The moral of this account is not lost by the report that during the performance the bassoon-player miscounted his bars and failed to come in at all.

The lack of artistic integrity behind such suppression of instruments is carried to extraordinary lengths, and we are all familiar with versions of first-rate musical works churned out by the queerest of incomplete combinations. Those responsible for such betrayals of music suffer from a rabid commercialism allied to a curious belief that when each note of the score is accounted for they are giving the listeners the essentials of the work performed. This is only an exaggerated form of the lack of sensitiveness which leads the conductor of a symphony orchestra to re-score works in order to eliminate certain rarer instruments. We are rather disarmed in our criticism of this disregard of the proprieties by the fact that many modern composers have permitted the publication of arrangements of their works for any combination ranging from an incomplete orchestra to a mouth-organ and pianoforte. Since we can hardly accuse the composers themselves of lack of sensitiveness where their own music is concerned, the blame must be laid at the door of the commercial attitude to music to which the insecure and ill-rewarded condition of the 'music makers' has led them. It is thus even more regrettable.

We are not yet at the end of the list of crimes which may be committed against the score of a composer, alive or dead.

Some conductors, for reasons best known to themselves, decide that a particular composition is too long, or that it contains passages which are not essential to the work as a whole. They therefore hack at the score, cut out a section or two, and present the maimed work to an unsuspecting public as the composer's own. In order to make the truncated piece of music hang together it is sometimes necessary to change a few chords, to insert a note or two, or to make some other adjustment, but this causes no qualms of conscience. The Olympian judgement of the conductor claims the right to improve on the form ill-advisedly chosen by the composer.

As in the other cases of maltreatment which I have mentioned, there may be an apparent justification. Some composers are over-fond of repeating what they have already stated at full length, but such faults are no less characteristic than the virtues. The Symphony in C major of Schubert was, according to Schumann, of 'heavenly length'; to a listener less fond of the Viennese composer's endless flow of inspiration or verbosity the work may become tiresome; but Schubert designed it like that, for his genius did not lie in succinct statement: he liked leisure in which to extend himself and his ideas.

There are, of course, instances where the composer, on second thoughts, or in response to the criticism of others, decided that he had been a trifle long-winded, and has authorized a shortening of his work. This was so with the Fifth Symphony of Tchaikovsky, but we may be wrong in presuming that the composer had done the best thing for his work in following the advice of others. Indeed, many conductors still prefer to perform the original version. As regards the Fourth Symphony of this composer, and many works by other men, there is no authority for the cuts and alterations which have become customary with certain conductors.

A flagrant case is that of Moussorgsky, whose *Boris Godunov* has become the classic instance of a musical work being changed and adapted to satisfy standards to which he himself had no intention of conforming. An earlier com-

position, *A Night on the Bare Mountain*, met a similar fate, not
at the hands of a later conductor, but of a colleague. Soon
after it was written, the composer wrote to Rimsky-
Korsakov and to Balakirev; to the former he said: 'I'm not
going to start altering it; with whatever shortcomings it was
born, it will have to live . . .'; to Balakirev he insisted: 'I
shall not alter either the general plan or the working out . . .
I will change nothing but the use of the percussion, which
is bad.' Yet Rimsky-Korsakov revised and re-orchestrated
the work and conducted the new version five years after the
death of the composer, and this is how the work is usually
presented to the public to-day. When the musician whose
work is in question has shown the independence and originality of a Moussorgsky, are we to be satisfied with the
bourgeoisified version of a smaller personality?

The music of Delius often proves an exception to much of
what has been said above, and if a careful listener observes
that four horns cover the parts allotted to six in the score he
need not be unduly disturbed. Delius was not very practical
when it came to the instrumentation of his compositions and
many of them were prepared for publication by other people
during his lifetime. He aimed at colour effects, and these
can sometimes be secured by simpler and less extravagant
means. But at all times the greatest care must be taken, for
an apparently innocuous change may result in a lamentable
loss of effect. It is then that the listener should remember
Berlioz.

Much more might be said on this matter, and some
pointed remarks of Sir Thomas Beecham, taken from an
article which he published in 1935, approach the problem
from a fresh angle:

Great masterpieces, or, indeed, any works of art, are in the first
instance the property of those who created them. In the case of a
painter his work is usually sold to a buyer: and what does the latter
proceed to do with it? He hangs it up somewhere and protects it

with all possible care. What he certainly does not do, unless he be a certifiable lunatic, is to repaint it here or there, or otherwise deface it; nor does he cut it up into a dozen pieces for distribution among other similarly afflicted unfortunates.

The pictures in our national collections are preserved and guarded in like manner, and the whole world can look at them, thus indulging the sense of proprietorship it enjoys in them. But I have never heard it suggested that any part owner is entitled to try his hand at touching up some master-work or obliterating any part of it which does not appeal to his taste. We all know that if he attempted any such thing he would speedily find himself in the nearest police station.

Later in the same article he sums up the whole matter in a way which leaves no more to be said:

Masterpieces are masterpieces, and remain such upon the one condition that they are seen or heard as designed by their creator. Arbitrarily altered by a lesser intelligence they at once cease to be masterpieces. It must be clear that the plea for altering great works to suit the taste of the 'whole world' is nothing more than the admission that they are above its comprehension. And behind this demand is concealed the envy of the lesser intelligence, which longs to drag down rare and exalted things from their high estate to its own petty level.

6 *The Perfect Orchestra*

(a)

In Amsterdam, Berlin, Boston, and Brussels, without going through the alphabet for other capitals and leading cities, the existence of a permanent orchestra is taken for granted. Indeed, it is the centre of their musical culture, which would suffer sadly if the orchestra disappeared. Nearer home, we have similar organizations in a number of towns. Since 1942–3 they have been established in Manchester, Liverpool, Birmingham, Leeds, Bournemouth, and Scotland, and although Wales is still without one it will have to make up the lack before long if it is to escape from the more narrow culture of choral singing.

London, however, presents its own problem. It has a permanent orchestra, of course, in the London Philharmonic, but the principle behind permanency is still rejected by a not unimportant body of opinion. Some members of that body may be disregarded as having other than purely musical reasons for their obstinacy, but when a fervent supporter of the L.P.O., for example, questions the validity of the principle, and in particular the justification of all the expense involved, a consideration of the positive advantages of the permanent orchestra seems worth while. For in spite of the progress being made in other centres, London is still the musical centre of England; it still attracts foreign musicians who believe big money can be made here, and is still the most likely place for the commercial exploitation of music. *Ad hoc* orchestras come and go in London, with an amazing resilience and with a remarkable duplication of players, but survive by exception. The conditions which make them easy to build render their foundations unreliable. They rely on the whims of fortune and the chances of individual initiative, and disappear when either ceases to be favourable. A secure and progressive musical culture needs stronger scaffolding.

The management and administration of a permanent orchestra is a much more complicated affair than that of the loosely knit organizations I have mentioned. Whereas the latter seldom go beyond the acceptance of engagements offered them, under the guidance of any conductor who is brought along, every detail of the permanent body needs to be carefully planned inside the framework of a full-time schedule which, while keeping the musicians fully occupied and bringing in as good an income as is consistent with a high artistic standard, must conform to a progressive pattern.

This pattern has two aspects. The musical one must ensure that the players have the finest artistic experiences possible; they must play with the leading conductors, prepare programmes which develop their musical and technical outlook and, by means of regular rehearsal together, acquire a team spirit and a collective understanding which guarantee a good performance no matter who the conductor may be. Indeed, the test of a fine orchestra is that it can give an excellent account of a programme even when the conductor is lacking in the essential qualities.

The other aspect is the social one. This comes from the need to create a schedule of concerts which will leave no weeks without the revenue needed to meet budgetary demands. Concerts must therefore be given, not only in the centre of the orchestra's city, but in the suburbs, the outlying districts and, occasionally, in provincial and foreign towns. But in finding new halls and new audiences it is not enough to make hurried and unregulated descents upon this town or that. For a short time this may bring golden returns, but no steady support will be secured, and results will never be more than speculative. The interest of the orchestra soon becomes, therefore, the interest of the public. This means that a certain number of the most sympathetic centres will be chosen to form the orchestral itinerary. In these centres the interest of all musical sections will be attracted by every method possible, and in time a steady public will be created which will justify the orchestra's work, financially and culturally.

When these visits are made in an organized circuit, the question of programme-building and of rehearsals takes on a new aspect, for now it is reasonable to prepare a number of programmes with adequate rehearsal, repeating them here and there over a certain period. The cost of the rehearsals, spread over the number of performances, becomes relatively light, although for any single performance it might well be prohibitive.

But however well-planned such visits to smaller centres may be, they will result in financial loss. That a permanent orchestra can carry them out more efficiently, at a higher standard and, ultimately, more economically, does not answer the question. Yet with even modest assistance from the authorities concerned, they can be financially justified. If such concerts were planned with an *ad hoc* orchestra, they would cost more or, alternatively, suffer from insufficient preparation and a lower standard. The engagement of a permanent conductor will add to the advantages, for he will be able to give to the general artistic plan a line of continuity which would otherwise be lacking; the public, too, will give its confidence to one director, who should then be able to lead it away from the beaten track of hackneyed programmes. The extra funds will not come in from the box-office. Our *ad hoc* tradition came from this fact in the past, and to-day the box office shows an even more distant relationship to overhead costs. These are substantially increased with the issue of contracts to a body of players, who must be guaranteed a weekly salary in return for an exclusive claim on their services.

Rehearsals, too, cannot be the subject of economies, or the whole justification of the orchestra is lost. Three, four, or even five rehearsals for an important performance take away any possibility of making ends meet, and it is not surprising that most commercial promoters look with a kindlier eye on an orchestra prepared to risk its standards and its reputation by accepting an engagement with one rehearsal. But although the amazing sight-reading powers of our players enable them to 'get by' under such an arrangement, this very facility threatens the development of a true, characteristic style of playing which distinguishes the world's best orchestras. Brilliant individual performances directed by a capable conductor will often fox the critic into believing he has heard the real thing, but they will never make up for the solid team-work, often with less good material, by which the world's most famous combinations have been built.

A fine orchestra does not rest on brilliant individuals. In England we have the outstanding example of the Hallé which, by the nature of its situation, cannot attract the leading players into its ranks. Yet, by intelligently directed rehearsal, and the maintenance of a consistent standard of performance, Barbirolli has developed a team spirit and a style which convince its critics. The L.P.O., since 1939, has had to abjure its former policy of pinning its faith to a few star artists, and has reached its present international standard of performance by its emphasis on team-work. The ideal combination of old experienced men and a high proportion of young ones, rehearsing and playing together on about 280 days a year, with a conductor whose training abilities are equal to the task, will more easily produce the highest results.

It will be seen that the task of planning and guiding such work is no light one, and the staff of a permanent orchestra is likely to be large and expensive. If the players are to be knit into a well-integrated body, their welfare demands continual attention. In these days of National Health, P.A.Y.E., pension funds, and sickness benefits, the accounts department will not merely have to cope with the normal matters involved in concert giving. And concerts in various centres, negotiations with Government and municipal authorities, arranging contracts with soloists and conductors, will all occupy administrative time. The planning of tours, publicity, the printing of posters and programmes demand a special staff to cover work which in earlier days would have been carried out by an agent on commission. That method would be unsatisfactory to-day.

The co-ordination of all these activities must rest in the hands of a governing committee which clearly sees the policy to be adopted, the policy which presents to the public something beyond mere concert giving, and to the players something more than a job. Once the inner co-ordination is reached the permanent orchestra can exert a strong influence on behalf of composers, young soloists, young listeners, and on the whole of the new generation.

The question of young players is most important to this discussion. Schools of instrumental playing already exist, as we know, but the application of the knowledge gained there to the conditions of the orchestra must be learned separately. It is doubtful whether this can be done anywhere but in the orchestra itself. It is not merely a question of getting to know the symphonic repertoire, of being able to follow a conductor, or of acquiring the subtle sensitiveness which makes perfect ensemble work a possibility. There is still the problem of playing in public, for which no amount of school work will be an adequate preparation; it must be learnt under the conditions of concert-giving, and therefore in the orchestra itself. How better, indeed, can a young musician fit himself for his task than in the ranks of a permanent orchestra where, among his older colleagues, he will find a repository of knowledge and experience, an example to follow and a craftsmanship to share. If one single argument were needed to justify the permanent organization of an orchestra, its scope as a training ground for young players would provide it. Unless we can pass these qualities on to the young men as they come along there is no hope for the great orchestra for which we are waiting. And if London fails to create it, we can hardly look to the rest of the country to repair our faults.

The prime advantage of a permanent orchestra is that it solves once and for all the problems of the deputy system, a system which alone held back the development of orchestral playing in this country for half a century. This deputy system has a short-term advantage for the player himself, for he can pick and choose his engagements, with little responsibility beyond pushing his own income to the highest level. But the acceptance of it by those who promote orchestras results in their bargaining for the services of known players to an extent which can demoralize, and is at present demoralizing, the whole profession. Many players will not only dispute this, but will argue that indeed they have no responsibility for its cause or cure. In an insecure world they feel no inclination to sacrifice their present interests for the future of music as a whole, and are cynical towards any suggestion that they are enjoying a short life, if a merry one.

These objections are understandable, and would soon disappear in an intelligently organized profession. Those put forward by conductors who have failed to secure the services of a permanent orchestra, critics who prefer the esoteric pleasure of brilliant but isolated performances to the steady educational work which is called for at the present time, and promoters who are satisfied to engage an orchestra only if it is willing to give the minimum of rehearsal, must be taken more seriously. For in solving the deputy problem, heavy expense is involved. Unless you can guarantee to a player willing to forsake hawking his services round to the highest bidder, an income on which he can live with some decency, he is bound to go on playing the old game, and we shall soon be back into the pre-1930's when English orchestral playing was as bad as its component individuals were good.

To avoid that, a new approach to many problems must be considered, and I deal with some of these problems in the next section of this chapter.

(*b*)

SOME time before the war I wrote an article in which I sketched, partly from imagination and partly from experience, the framework of what I called the 'perfect orchestra'. It was then no more than a day-dream of mine, for what influence could a mere viola-player (with no ambitions of becoming a conductor) have upon the development of the august and aristocratic London Philharmonic Orchestra?

When the unexpected happened, it was interesting to observe to what extent my day-dream had been prophetic, and in what way my original ideas had to be adapted in the light of subsequent experience. Even the L.P.O. is not yet the perfect orchestra, and will not be until the society which surrounds it ceases to place prohibitions and difficulties in its way. But many of the problems with which organizers of symphony orchestras are faced could be solved to-day, despite current adverse conditions, and it is for this reason that they are exposed again here.

In principle, most of the hopes I expressed, and the improvements I suggested, have proved practicable, even where present unsettled circumstances have made their full realization impossible. On the other hand, some were too modest, and the experience of eleven years' work under new conditions has left the original thesis far behind. In the pages which follow I shall make no attempt to compare vague plans with concrete realizations, for I do not wish to justify myself as a prophet, but I shall endeavour to show what has been done and what must still be done to build the ideal instrument for orchestral performances. For an orchestra must be considered as an instrument, a great organ with every stop and every pedal a living being, with a will, a taste, and an artistic conscience of its own.

Let us clear the air at once by admitting that such an orchestra could never succeed as a commercial proposition. Were that possible, we should have had at least one perfect orchestra already, but the fact that it will cost the community money to hear justice done to the greatest musical compositions of the world need disturb no one. A nation which for a long time has considered it worth while to grant reasonably heavy subsidies to such institutions as art galleries, museums, libraries, and so on (to mention only the more useful and non-destructive recipients of public monies) will not boggle at the comparatively small sums which will make orchestral music safe for democracy.

It is indeed curious that public money is voted not unreadily to the various still-life forms of culture mentioned above, while considerable unwillingness is shown where the living body of an orchestra is concerned. This could be understood if the public demand for the first exceeded that for the second, but each of our leading permanent orchestras plays to nearly 250,000 people annually (without counting those who listen to broadcast performances), while the Promenade Season at the Royal Albert Hall breaks attendance records each year. Are any museums, art galleries, or libraries regularly besieged in this way? The National Gallery, with its war-time musical activity, and the recent exhibition of the works of Van Gogh at the Tate Gallery, are special exceptions.

Yet it is not merely a question of money. The B.B.C. Symphony Orchestra has since its foundation been subsidized in a hitherto unprecedented manner, but it does not yet fulfil the demands of the ideal orchestra. I do not wish to subject this body to any detailed criticism; if my suggestions prove valid they will show clearly in which ways the founders of this great musical organization have failed to achieve what they must, consciously or unconsciously, have been aiming at. The financial question is at this moment a separate issue with which I shall deal later on in these pages.

Our first duty is to select the players. How is this done nowadays in our best orchestras? Players reach their seats on the platform of the leading concert halls by a variety of methods, as befits our twentieth-century confusion of anarchy for democracy. A player may be the obvious choice for the vacant position, he may be recommended or given an audition, or he may gain the coveted place by even more devious methods. To avoid introducing acrimony into the discussion, let us consider only the more regular means of arrival. Recommendation is sometimes satisfactory and sometimes quite the reverse. If the authority whose work is accepted is of known integrity and qualified to make such a suggestion the results are usually good, but when other than artistic motives come into play the orchestra may be saddled with a mere passenger or worse, for with the best will in the world it is sometimes difficult to avoid the temptation of thinking more highly of the qualifications of one's friends than of strangers.

The audition is a favourite, but by no means exclusive,

method of judging new material for some of our leading concerns, but by itself it is nevertheless one of the least satisfactory. Auditions are not always genuine. Where the constitution of an organization is so framed that all vacancies must be offered for public competition, it is not unusual for the audition to be a sort of cruel make-believe, the competitors being unaware that the post for which they are straining every nerve has already been filled behind the scenes. I could quote more than one instance of this, but, in any case, the mere suggestion that one or two musicians are so perspicacious that they can judge in ten minutes the player's aptitude for the involved duties of an orchestral career is completely absurd, and is rightly regarded as being so by all players of experience. A musician who is sensitive enough to respond to the subtly expressed wishes of a conductor may well lack the boldness which will carry an inferior player through an audition with flying colours.

For many years before the war the Berlin Philharmonic Orchestra employed the method of public audition for choosing new members. At each audition the conductor, Wilhelm Furtwängler, was present, supported by the members of the whole orchestra. The newcomer played, and was given full consideration and allowance for the effect of nervousness which such an ordeal must cause. His achievements were then discussed by the conductor and the orchestral musicians until some approximation of his worth was arrived at. It is said that agreement was invariably reached on lines suggested by Dr Furtwängler to his colleagues. When such a method is carried out sincerely it will avoid the worst features of the system, but one hears that, at one difficult period in the orchestra's fight for existence, the Mayor of Berlin attended auditions, reducing them to nothing more than a formality. This attempt to interfere, although perhaps well intended, was not taken seriously and proved to be a failure.

Nevertheless, those in charge of an orchestra must get some conception of a new player's aptitude, and if an audition is regarded as a first step no harm is done. In the post-war London Philharmonic Orchestra a player is heard, first of all, by all the directors with a knowledge of the instrument concerned, with any others who care to attend. The conductor is often called in as well. It is rare that a player is offered a contract as the immediate result of an audition, the usual method being to suggest a month's trial in the orchestra. This has proved to be a valuable precaution, for more than once a player who has made an excellent impression when playing alone has shown himself quite unsuited to meet the particular demands of playing regularly with the Orchestra. On the other hand, some of those who were obviously overcome by the task of playing before a group of hardened professionals have fallen into place with no difficulty during the month's trial. In this way a high proportion of young players has been found and guided towards the serious career of an orchestral player.

Still more of these young players are, however, found wanting, and new methods must be devised. We must know where to put our hands on our future players. Where are they found to-day? The existing methods of recruiting players in England having previously been disposed of, an alternative must be submitted. This is, that young musicians must be tested in such a way that their all-round qualifications are displayed and given full scope. It must not be forgotten that the personality and general culture of a musician are of no less importance than his technical equipment. An orchestra as a whole is greater than the sum of its parts, and from being a mere collection of instrumentalists it becomes, by a judicious dovetailing of the units, a corporate body. This is the more so in a permanent orchestra, where the players spend the greater part of their waking lives together, and where one or two misfits may prejudice the happiness, welfare, and standard of the whole body.

In actual fact, the training offered by our schools of music has been primarily directed towards producing soloists. So much so that Sir Thomas Beecham once referred to a distinguished orchestra as 'this collection of disappointed soloists'. Such direction of official training is no more, one imagines, than a relic of the past, when the number of students was small, when the study of music was little more than a social accomplishment, and when, in any case, it was generally accepted that such orchestras as did exist were composed largely of foreign players. These considerations have long ceased to be valid. The first world war led to the disappearance of foreign orchestral players, and to the creation of a profession of our own, and the development of the silent film up to the end of the twenties brought into being a large body of professional instrumentalists. That was the period when the schools of music might have brought their curriculum up to date, but little was done beyond the weekly, or bi-weekly, orchestral rehearsal, during which a number of works – too frequently concertos – were summarily disposed of. So that a brilliant student might leave his studies with a few concertos under his arm and with supreme confidence in his future as a soloist. In those days he would be lucky if he secured a position in a small orchestra playing in a cinema or hotel; otherwise he might make a desperate living training others for a career in which he himself had lost faith. As an exception, he might have obtained a seat in a real orchestra, only to find that his rather expensive education had left such *lacunae* in his knowledge that, for the first twelve months or so, he was little more than a passenger. If he were skilful in lying low he might survive and become an orchestral player; if not, one of the careers mentioned above would swallow him up.

Since 1945 the situation has changed considerably; for

the better as far as the immediate interests of the individual musician are concerned, but perhaps less so for the future of our orchestras. The demands made for the services of orchestral players by the film and gramophone studios, the radio, and by the many symphony orchestras established in different parts of the country have temporarily outstripped the supply, and it is safe to say that no musician of any qualification need be without a diary full of engagements. This is, doubtless, a satisfactory situation, in keeping with an official policy of full employment; but it has dangerous by-products, especially for the younger player. It is often possible for a young player to secure an important position as soon as his studies are completed, or even earlier, and he often concludes that he has no more to learn. As he will receive the same salary or fees as his much older and more experienced colleagues he may well be tempted to see life through distorted spectacles, to the subsequent detriment of his whole career. Money may become far more significant to him than music, and he may never conceive that his work is primarily a public service and not a simple commercial activity.

For the older players similar dangers exist. They were brought up in a hard school, and spent most of their youthful years going from pillar to post, or from pier to playhouse, picking up their professional experience *en route*. The more talented of them made their way eventually into the inner circle of those who play for 'small combinations', and whose incomes were in inverse order to the musical value of the works they performed. While such a career may prove profitable, it subjects a player to an endless round of engagements which plays havoc with his nerves and consequently with his standard of performance. Too often, such players end by regarding music as a job like any other, thus revealing a lamentable frame of mind quite unsuited to the demands made by the best in music. If we are to have the finest possible orchestra, these men must be brought in before they have been spoiled by the purely commercial side of life.

This anarchic treatment of available talent is unsatisfactory from many points of view. I do not wish to convey the impression that there is no opening for soloists and chamber-musicians; on the contrary, more quartets and similar ensembles succeed in finding a living than ever before in this country. This is an encouraging sign, but activities of this kind can absorb only a small number of our most talented players while orchestral playing – in addition to being one of the most satisfying branches of the musical profession – offers, or should offer, the most secure and lasting activity, and could provide a future for large numbers of musicians. An orchestra itself needs these players when they are young and enthusiastic, and should not have to wait until the struggle for existence has dulled the sensibilities, weakened the juvenile vitality, and created the pains of an inferiority complex. But this is what has happened for many years, and orchestral playing as an art has suffered.

We must base our plans on existing organizations, and the weekly orchestral practices held at most of our leading schools of music can become the focal point. These are normally directed by one of our better-known conductors, whose long experience with professional orchestras enables him to obtain a passable collective result, but who cannot be expected, in the time allowed him, to enter into problems of instrumental difficulties, even if his technical knowledge enabled him to do so. It is clear then that the students attending such rehearsals should be given the opportunity between each rehearsal of preparing the works to be undertaken. This is not merely a question of taking the parts home for private practice, for many a passage carefully prepared alone will go sadly astray when the psychological moment in the orchestra arrives. In this way are 'band-room' soloists often betrayed.

For efficient preparation, the student needs the active presence of other players. He must develop the sixth sense of ensemble playing which neither conscientious counting nor a watchful eye on the conductor's baton will replace. He must learn the hundred-and-one points which are all the more important because they do not appear in the score. He must study, in short, the craft of orchestral playing in addition to the craft of his instrument, and for this he will often look in vain to his own professor, whose experience in the orchestra is frequently of the slightest.

The staff of each of our schools should therefore be enlarged to include one or more old, experienced orchestral musicians who can pass on to the younger generation the fruits of their many years at one famous concert hall or another. Certain players I have in mind would not be unwilling to forsake the charms of sitting at the feet of conductors, or of playing their *n*th performance of this or that symphony. The conductor of the school orchestra would find it difficult to present such hardened players with an unfamiliar score. During the week preceding the rehearsal, a number of classes could be held, various sections of the orchestra being dealt with in turn, and in conjunction with others, until each player would be familiar not only with his own part, but with those of his colleagues, and his place in the general scheme could become clear in a way which might never be possible during the actual rehearsal. This is, after all, similar to the plan followed by a symphony orchestra in creating its own standard and style of performance, and is merely the logical method of reaching these results. Students of such a course would naturally be expected to attend the rehearsals and concerts given by the leading symphony orchestras, and some agreement might easily be made to facilitate such attendance.

A simple extension of this scheme could lead naturally to a form of orchestral apprenticeship. The Musicians' Union might not at first be convinced of the validity of this scheme, for the possibilities of exploiting the apprentice would not be few, and orchestral organizations are always chary of accepting inexperienced players into their ranks. I have already indicated some of the dangers which might result from a haphazard search for experience; but there is no reason, apart from the financial one, why such young players should not be attached to an orchestra and given the opportunity of becoming well-equipped musicians before being called upon to shoulder the full responsibilities of a permanent position. The preparation classes mentioned above would not fail to reveal any outstanding talent, and if a sympathetic *liaison* existed between schools of music and our orchestras the whole of the orchestral personnel might well be recruited from this source.

The normal practice has led in the past to restricting opportunities for young promising men on the ground that they lacked the essential experience; it was no less effective in preventing them from getting precisely that experience. Since the war, when the supply of musicians for the relatively low-paid services of a symphony orchestra seldom satisfies the demand, the position has sometimes been reversed, and we have had the spectacle of a young player being given the full responsibilities of a leading position, and finding the strain of facing up to world-famous conductors so great that the actual job of playing his instrument became more than he could manage. It has also enabled us, particularly in the London Philharmonic, to reveal unusual talent which, before the war, would have had no opportunity of developing.

A series of scholarships, designed to cover the expenses of such apprenticeships, should be instituted and would act as a valuable incentive, not only in the later orchestral classes, but throughout the student's career. He would feel that orchestral playing offered a future worthy of his most serious efforts – and until we have succeeded in giving that prestige to the symphony orchestra, we shall have failed in one of our most compelling tasks.

These schemes would demand a happy co-ordination between the schools of music and the managing bodies of symphony orchestras. Without this it would be difficult for teaching organizations to find the ideal men for the coaching posts, and the normal flow of the most successful students into the orchestra would be checked. But such a scheme would have striking and beneficial effects on the standard and prestige of the orchestral profession, and difficulties would certainly not come from that side. It must be said regretfully that our schools show little readiness for co-operation along these lines, and when a student, a few months before his graduation, secures by his own initiative a position in a symphony orchestra, he is frequently regarded as a lost soul at the school, while the orchestra is looked upon as a body snatcher.

Apprenticeships would, of course, be possible only where the positions to which they led were secure, and where the salaries were sufficiently high and progressive to make the player disinclined to wish for change. One peculiarity of the orchestral profession is that, in general, a young man, once having justified himself in a position, is likely to earn the highest fees or salary of his lifetime. He is thus in the opposite position from, let us say, a young doctor who, after many years of study, will earn at first little more than a capable typist, but who can look forward to steady and considerable increases which will ensure a comfortable middle age and a retirement free from care. The dangerous position where the young man is extremely well paid before he has realized the value of money, and has little chance of increasing his income as his private responsibilities increase, and when, indeed, his skill may be declining, can hardly be corrected in present circumstances; but one imagines that with the proper support of orchestras, the establishment of pension schemes and other safeguards, conditions similar to those of other well-ordered professions might be introduced here.

The conditions of a post in an orchestra would need to be such that it would be no less unnecessary than it was undesirable for the musicians to accept outside engagements, with the exception of solo work and chamber music. To-day it is difficult to enforce such a rule, for the comparison between what a player may earn in a recognized orchestra with what can be gained in the free-lance world is so unfavourable that those with heavy responsibilities or a high regard for money can only be retained at the cost of a certain understanding latitude. But it is a handicap to an orchestra aiming at the highest standards, and should be made obviously unnecessary.

Considerations of security bring us to the question of pensions, which has been inconclusively debated from time to time, and is still only answered in exceptional cases. Any orchestra which fails to provide an adequate pension scheme for its personnel will always be faced with the various problems caused by uncertainty of the future, to which musicians are even more exposed than most other workers. A constantly changing personnel will wreck any orchestra, and deny it the virtues of a truly permanent organization.

The chief argument brought against pensions (apart from the financial difficulty which will be dealt with later) is that it would deprive the profession of the 'salutary' element of risk which alone persuades the orchestral player to give of his best. This is a calumny on a class of people who, even in the exact wording of a B.B.C. contract, are referred to as 'artists'. It would also be a reflection on the wisdom of those responsible for the selection of musicians who, if they satisfied the high standards we have set, could be relied upon to behave as artists and not as piece-workers. If security and pensions have such a devastating effect on the human conscience, it is difficult to understand why they are always awarded to our leading public servants, from the Lord Chief Justice to college professors. When Tchehov makes one of his characters say: 'You know yourself that an uncertain position has a great tendency to make people apathetic,' he is showing more respect for, and understanding of, human nature than are the opponents of pensions for musicians. Yet little has so far been done in this direction. It is indeed curious that we should need to discuss the principle of the matter in the middle of the twentieth century. Almost a hundred years ago, Nicolai, the conductor of the Vienna Philharmonic Orchestra, was regretting the difficulties of inaugurating such a scheme, and it was not long before something was done, and the last concert of the season, called the Nicolai-Konzert, was given for the benefit of a pension fund.

The L.P.O. Committee, as one of its first actions, went into the question of a pension fund. The Royal Philharmonic Society devoted the proceeds of a concert to this purpose, and several private donations laid the foundations of a fund, but the matter was complicated and difficult. No member of the Orchestra doubted the necessity or desirability of such a provision, but the limitations of the period and other urgent financial demands delayed the realization of the scheme. It was not until 1949, after three years' generous support from the London County Council, that the L.P.O. Pension Fund came into being on the normal contributory basis, helped on its way by the advice of two L.C.C. experts. The full effect of this noteworthy step will not be felt for some years, but its stabilizing influence cannot be doubted.

It must be admitted at once that – pensions or no pensions – there is a danger of deterioration in any established organization. The greatest vigilance must be exercised in finding and rooting out the real causes. To avoid stagnation, some feeling of progress must always be present, and a flat rate of salary, or one with a tendency to decline, is therefore harmful. An annual increase of some kind, avoiding the inevitable feeling of injustice in an old player when he sees the newcomer starting his career at the same rates, and offering, too, the possibilities of disciplinary control, would act as a valuable stimulus. An endless series of concerts, and of rehearsals for rehearsals' sake, are primarily causes of flagging interest, and while the former danger is unlikely in a non-commercial orchestra, the latter, were the organization to come under any sort of bureaucratic control, would be only too probable. There should be nothing vague about a rehearsal; it should have a clear objective and not be used as practice for a conductor, or as a disciplinary measure. It is the boredom of pointless rehearsals which so frequently dulls the edge of orchestral playing. This is largely the responsibility of the conductor, who must be chosen for the perfect orchestra with the utmost care. I have dealt earlier in these pages with these delicate problems and can only hope that when the day comes for the formation of the ideal organization a more fearless attitude to these questions will prevail. In the meantime I am convinced that in seeking to explain lack of discipline and enthusiasm among certain groups of musicians, the correct reasons are seldom given. I have always found that when programmes are well chosen, the conductor's sincerity and capabilities beyond doubt, and the players kept well informed of the reasons behind difficult conditions, no serious trouble will occur. Musicians want passionately to enjoy their work, and will do so naturally unless enjoyment is prevented.

It is a curious fact with musicians, and perhaps similarly with other folk, that while they grumble at forced orchestral rehearsals for which they may be well paid, they will devote themselves to a chamber-music ensemble which may put them to considerable expense of time and money. I regard this paradox as a healthy reaction in an artist, and one which has a moral for those who consider musicians to have mercenary minds. If the interest is kept alive, not only in the music, but in the whole organization of the orchestra, enthusiasm will not fail.

The mention of chamber music brings up another point of great importance. Orchestral playing without the corrective of private practice will inevitably deteriorate, as for the rank-and-file player there is insufficient personal responsibility and little call upon self-reliance. There is no better antidote to this danger than chamber music, and the members of the perfect orchestra should be constrained to spend a regular amount of time in this way, and their duties should be arranged with this necessity in mind. In addition to acquiring that sense of individual responsibility, players will develop that faculty of listening which goes farther towards obtaining an excellent orchestral ensemble than any amount of concentration on the conductor's baton will do. But the players must be given ample leisure for such private work, and there must be no possibility that the story I once heard in Germany should be true of any instrumentalist of our orchestra.

A viola player (it would be!) in one of the many municipal orchestras there was retiring after forty years' service. His colleagues gave him a worthy send-off, after which he tucked his instrument-case contentedly under his arm and made his way home. At the house door he was greeted by his wife, whom he had married shortly after his appointment to the orchestra. 'Here you are at last,' she said, 'but whatever have you got under your arm?' 'Oh, that's my viola,' replied her husband. 'Really,' she said, 'I've often heard you speak about it, but it's the first time I have ever seen you with it.'

The internal life of an orchestra must be so organized that each member feels that he is a living part of the whole. Differences of treatment for principals (apart from the obvious one of salaries) should be avoided whenever possible, so that no class division may be created. I heard recently of a case where on a long sea voyage the principals were given cabin accommodation, while the remainder went tourist. Certain misunderstandings and problems between the players, conductors, and directors are bound to occur from time to time, as must happen when a number of people are considering a question from many points of view. An elected orchestral committee will therefore be of great value, even if it is no more than a consultative body, provided that complete freedom of speech is observed, and that it will not be regarded cynically as a piece of window-dressing calculated to keep the players quiet. Through such a committee, the orchestra would become articulate and many details which caused dissatisfaction would be corrected. The recognition of the Musicians' Union by governing bodies is most necessary and to-day is seldom questioned, for it is generally understood that this organization has, like them, the interest of music and the musical profession seriously at heart, even if, in its day-to-day work, it is sometimes forced to take a short view of various problems.

Even better, however, than an external management and a consultative committee is the completely democratic system, whereby the orchestra is organized and controlled by its own members. Here, not only will absolute freedom of speech be guaranteed, thus enabling the elected committee to profit by the criticism and advice which members of the orchestra may proffer, but any attempt to override such criticism can be immediately checked and wrong policies corrected. An organization of this kind will inevitably proceed by trial and error, but if a frank exchange of views and opinions exists between the committee and the orchestra neither will travel far from the right road. Past insecurities have tended to accentuate the mercenary side of musicians' characters, and being artists, children of the moment, they are often tempted to take the obvious but short-sighted view of any problem. Nevertheless, their loyalty to anything which is honestly explained to them and which catches their imagination is easily gained, although the older hand is *rusé* and will not be deceived by fluent verbiage.

Similar instances could certainly be quoted elsewhere. It is worth placing on record the devotion of members of the London Philharmonic since the war when, during a most despairing and unprofitable period, certain players did not hesitate to decline highly-paid contracts in order to remain loyal to their orchestra as an institution. It is extremely doubtful whether any outside employer could have commanded such loyalty. The spreading of the idea that the interests of the orchestra are something greater than those of individuals comprising it might be taken as a dangerous advocacy of totalitarianism, but for the strength of the constitution, which lies in moulding the history and activities of the orchestra with due regard for its individual members and in creating a balance between the demands of music as an art and the exigencies of everyday life. It has to be remembered that those responsible for the early years of a permanent orchestra are laying foundations of an organization which will be active when every present member is forgotten, and the day-to-day problems have to be solved against the wider canvas of the stretching future. It will be seen that conscientious service on an orchestral committee can be no less exciting than exacting!

The question of general culture has been absurdly neglected in the past, and the music colleges should take a greater interest and responsibility in this direction. While a single-track mind may be admirable and even necessary for the production of an outstanding virtuoso, it can be nothing more than a hindrance to the natural development of the type of player we are concerned with. The very nature of a musician's life will tend to separate him from the normal activities of the community, and his early education and his later opportunities must be organized with a view to counteracting this influence. When this is successfully achieved, the perfect orchestra will be a living body of artists, and not a mere collection of talented individuals whose gifts, through lack of wider expression, are often driven to death.

7 A Background to Music

TO-DAY we live in an age of specialization. Had Leonardo da Vinci, painter, scientist, musician, deviser of masques and ballets, experimental chemist, skilful dissector, and author of the first standard book on anatomy, lived in this century, he would have had to mend his ways and decide in which of these activities his direction lay. Any failure to make this choice would have exposed him to the label of dilettante or amateur and to the refusal of serious consideration for his works. The following story illustrates this – and other things. Richard Tauber, known in England as lieder, opera and, principally, musical comedy and light opera singer, began his career as a symphony orchestra conductor. In this capacity he appeared on many occasions with the L.P.O. My own opinion as to the great potentialities of Tauber as conductor has little importance here, but I was assailed by many people who considered that the L.P.O. Committee was taking part in what might be termed a lucrative 'stunt'. This attitude culminated in the remark of another conductor, who said, 'Oh, well! if this is how things are going, I shall have to sing at my next concert!' The obvious retort was not to be denied. 'Why not, if you can sing as well as Tauber!'

But life has become so complex that the temptation to plough one's own furrow and let the rest of the world roll by is almost too great to resist. Now while this may not affect the quality of the output of the technical worker, to whom, in these days of the division of labour, the means may be synonymous with the ends, it is fatal to the work of any artist, and particularly of the musician. With other arts the mere subject-matter is enough to keep the artist in touch with reality; even if the juxtaposition of objects in a surrealist painting presents a problem for the psycho-analyst, the work is at least representational. Only in music, the most abstract and therefore the most impressive of arts, can the complete divorce from reality become possible.

A musician must be a human being before he is an artist; his art must be the expression of his personal attitude to life. How will he acquire an attitude to life if his whole time is occupied with the problems of technique and the means of expression? No amount of technical brilliance or recondite knowledge will hide the paucity of emotion or intellect in an artist's make-up, as attendance at many recitals will show. Technique is no more than the alphabet and the words of an art, and it is only the difficulty of acquiring a satisfactory technique that has led so many of us astray. But along what a fatal path have we been led! How often are we told that the true artist must devote his whole energies to his art, without the realization that art is the highest expression of mankind and has value only in so far as it is enriched with the blood of life.

It is true that the abstract nature of music lends colour to the contention that it is something apart from life, dwelling in sacred isolation; but any study of musical history will prove that it is influenced, in common with general culture, by the forces which govern life. To avoid the sterility which must inevitably follow from any separation of music from the wider human interests, the musician must stretch forth his hands and gather the fruits of culture from the best of his predecessors and contemporaries. Felix Weingartner fully recognized this necessity when he said: 'I have often been reproached with many-sidedness. What is many-sidedness? To do honestly what one is capable of doing with a good conscience and not to hesitate in allowing one's capabilities to branch out in various ways, provided that the resultant branches are from the same tree.' That this was no idle phrase is amply shown by the books Weingartner published, books covering a wide field of interest outside music. His remark is in the true tradition of his master, Dr Wilhelm Mayer, who, as W. A. Rémy, taught Kienzl, Weingartner, Busoni, and von Reznicek. He used to say: '*Möglichst vielseitige Bildung macht den Künstler.*'

Many other examples of this breadth of cultural outlook might be quoted. Berlioz, Wagner, and numerous modern musicians have found time and enthusiasm to devote to the study of languages, politics, aesthetics, and the appreciation of another art. It may, however, be objected that while this is possible and even admirable for composers and conductors, there is no opportunity for such development in the life of the instrumental virtuoso, who by the very nature of his particular talent must take to music very early in life and devote the greater part of his formative years to the highly specialized study of his instrument. This certainly presents new problems, but none which is insuperable.

It may be a moot point whether Busoni fully realized himself as a composer, but as a virtuoso-pianist he fulfilled all his early promise. Liszt again, in spite of all his youthful travels and concerts, allowed full development to his wider interests, and the best of his influence can be traced to this general culture. There was wisdom in the decision that Yehudi Menuhin should forgo public appearances for a considerable period to allow time for other studies and normal mental development. This shows a healthy attitude to youthful talent which might be dwelt on by all who worship at the sign of the velvet jacket. There is no more artistic justification for musical prodigies than for performing monkeys. A little less finger gymnastics and a little more mental activity would enable many youthful virtuosos to survive their later encounters with the world.

Conductors, composers, and prodigies apart, there is still the ordinary professional musician to be considered. How many orchestral musicians do we know who regard their professional activities solely as a job with a certain amount of leisure to be spent in any pursuit demanding little or no mental effort? How many teachers to whom music means nothing more than a rather abstruse system of mathematics to be inflicted on helpless children who are never taught its connexion with an emotional art?

The principal of a famous British musical institution, when approached by a number of students with a request for permission to form a debating society, decided after two days of cogitation that he was quite in favour of such a society, provided that there should be no discussion on politics, religion, sex, or music. The gallant students attempted to form the club in spite of these disabilities, but their efforts were fruitless. The organization died from inanition when it was found that everything in which they were interested touched upon subjects which their principal had laid under a ban. This is a far cry from the counsels of W. A. Rémy, and is another indication of the tendency of our musical life to become a mere profession, a not unpleasant method of gaining a living, rather than a culture fulfilling the task of explaining a man's life to himself.

8 Interlude I
Instruments and Players

COMMENTING on an article which I once wrote for the *Musical Times*, Mr Ernest Newman remarked, 'Is there something in the viola that develops exceptional intelligence in its executants, or is it just that when a man has exceptional intelligence he takes up the viola as a matter of course?' The question is rather like the old trick of 'heads I win, tails you lose,' and embarrassed modesty can give no reply either way; but Mr Newman's rhetorical question does by implication suggest that certain instruments and certain types of mind and character go together. One can do no more than generalize rather lightly on the subject, for to everything I say someone will find a valid exception.

Viola players, it is true, are often 'sicklied o'er with the pale cast of thought'; as Bernard Shore once said, 'The violist is generally reflective with a touch of melancholy about him.' This is less true to-day than it was many years ago, when the orchestral parts which the poor viola player had to perform could be summed up by *oom-cha-cha*, the only variety offered coming from the relation between the numbers of *ooms* to those of *chas*. *Mais nous avons changé tout cela.* When Berlioz heard Paganini play the viola – we should probably shudder at it to-day – and wrote *Harold in Italy*, he opened up a path which led directly to Strauss and *Don Quixote*, reaching the heights of Lionel Tertis, from which the modern viola player can survey a wide field specially prepared for him, in which blooms a growing harvest of important works. He is no longer recruited from the ranks of unsuccessful and disappointed violinists; cases are even known of viola players who have never had preliminary training on the violin. Yet there is something about the melancholy, even morbid, tone of the instrument, its modest harmonic position in the middle of the orchestra, which does not fail to attract a serious cast of mind, or to influence in this manner the minds of those who adopt it as their instrument.

The first violins represent a great contrast to their more grave colleagues. Here we have the fiddle-players! To call them 'disappointed soloists' may be unkind, but it is true that many of them harbour hopes of holding the stage in this or that concerto, of which they faithfully believe they have a deeper understanding than Mischa X or Efrem Y. They are no less serious than viola players, but their more profound thoughts are directed less to a *Weltanschauung* than to the study of their instruments. Frequently, their career has presented them with fleeting opportunities of holding a baton, and a secret passion gnaws at their vitals to show their colleagues their mastery of the orchestra. When this is only a sentimental and rather highly-coloured glance backward there is little harm done, but when it is the capable leader who is bitten by the desire for conducting, it may well be that his foolish and misguided passion will end in disaster. For a first-rate leader is more rare than rubies, far more so than the commonplace conductor he would almost certainly become. Few cases exist of an orchestral leader turned great conductor. But first violins are lovably childish, and must be excused their dreams of greatness.

The seconds provide a temperamental justification of their position in the orchestra. They do not share the flashy qualities of their fellow violinists, nor are they followed by the suspicion of stodginess which marks their alto colleagues.

They are indeed a little indistinguishable, with no voice which can rightly be called their own, shyly supporting the brilliant work of their more self-conscious neighbours. Individually, they are less sanguine, less flamboyant, than the first violins, and seem rather disillusioned. There was a time when they had hoped to be placed immediately in the public eye, but now, crowded behind desks of music, they have lost their identity, and regret it.

The cellos are something of a problem. Like the first violins they are incorrigible individualists, each considering himself a soloist, and perhaps quite rightly. The singing, sentimental quality of the instrument has its counterpart in a rather romantic view of life. An untidy cellist is an exception, and their smart clothes, a certain loquacity, and good looks, often endear them to the fair sex. Exceptions? Yes, they are almost as common as the rule; I said they were something of a problem.

To complete the string family there are the double basses, who are the centre of a constant struggle between dignity and the grotesque. If every bass player were tall, broad, and muscular, on the pattern of a Life Guard or a City policeman, or even as well built as Adolf Lotter or Eugene Cruft, there would be little to say, for he would be a match for the massive wooden structure of which he is master. But Nature has no objection to a little incongruity, and can we be surprised if it finds its way into art? Certainly, the diminutive bass player, nobly struggling with his recalcitrant instrument, is by no means an exception. But for all that, bass players have a dignity which does not only derive from the essential part they play. As a race, they have more respect for their instruments than any other string players; 'the bass' is spoken of almost with awe. Perhaps it is because they are frequently craftsmen, and are kept busy applying their skill when their unwieldy instruments meet with mishaps in transit. It seems natural for them, too, to consider their own qualities as a section of the orchestra, rather than as individual players. They share the serious turn of mind found among viola players, but seem to turn their attention rather to the graphic arts.

One may wonder at this point what forces have driven certain players to their particular instruments. There is, of course, the classic instance of the horn player who, when asked why he had devoted his life to the study of the French horn, replied naïvely, 'Well, my father played the horn.' He must have realized that this was only half of the story, for taking the horse to the water does not compel him to drink. It is true that many boys who begin to study the instrument which their father has played so successfully, soon give it up through lack of interest or failure to make progress. Yet those who persevere and devote their lives to the study seldom fail to approach in some measure the type belonging to their particular instrument.

In general, and in student days in particular, there is a way of life of the various instrumentalists which cannot fail to have its effect. And there is the actual playing of the instrument. Players of the heavier brass instruments are rarely teetotal; they may go into training for an important season, but the deep sigh of relief when it is all over is usually the preparation for blowing the froth from a pint of beer. Wind players generally appreciate the pleasures of the convivial cup, but as string players – even to the staid violas – are little less appreciative, we are not provided with any valuable data.

Generally speaking, wind players have an air of superiority with regard to their string playing brethren, which is illustrated by the remark make by a horn player who was being chivvied by a violinist about a note he had cracked during the performance. Finding that none of the usual excuses and explanations satisfied the mocking violinist, the outraged horn player added, 'Well, anyway, I am a soloist and not a member of the chorus, like you!' Add to the truth of this statement the fact that the more responsible services of wind instrumentalists command greater financial recompense, and it will be seen that a tendency may exist to consider these star players as an upper class. In actual fact, musicians are such friendly folk that in an orchestra which plays together regularly any such imaginary or real class barriers cannot continue to separate them. On the other hand, they are not likely to be mistaken for string players; their whole bearing has a *je-ne-sais-quoi* which distinguishes them.

Horn players, for example, might pass for business men of the City, with their correct dress, their gravity of manner, and their well-built houses in the better suburbs. There is little of the vagrant musician about them; one feels that their bank balances are good and their life insurances sound. They are proud of their musical lineage, especially if they can trace it back to the great Adolf Borsdorf, and are no less proud to pass on the mystery of their craft to the younger generation at one of the reputable schools of music. That these qualities are recognized by their confrères is apparent from their election to orchestral committees; Adolf Borsdorf was a member of the original L.S.O. committee in 1904, and two members of the L.P.O. horn quartet (including a son of Borsdorf) served as Directors on the L.P.O. committee. Although many of them have spent part of their younger life attached to one of the leading Army bands, military life seems to have left no very deep mark on them, and their association with the colours has been more a stage in their career than an experience of its own. The very scarcity of good performers on this instrument has made it worth their while to buy themselves out before the stigma of the Staff band has become too apparent.

Not so the real brass players. Trumpets, trombones, and tuba represent, with a few exceptions, the soldier returned to civilization – and not liking it overmuch. They have little sympathy with what might be called 'modern' ideas, and secretly believe that a good dose of military discipline would do those unruly fiddle players a world of good. It is not for nothing that they play instruments which are meant to be heard, whose dominos resound throughout London, and whose mistakes cannot be erased. Their views are direct and intransigent; argument and verbosity are for the less masculine departments of the orchestra. But they are as simple as they are direct, and their loyalty is easily obtained when they feel they are getting a square deal – even when, in fact, they are not.

The wood-wind players are the true star artists, who rise brilliantly out of the anonymity of the orchestra, and who, with dazzling technique or well-turned phrases, win the approbation of their audiences and the rather dubious appreciation of the conductor who may feel that such glorious independence and originality constitute a threat to his personal sway. Temperamentally, they are allied to the first fiddles, with the same streak of exhibitionism and the same confidence in their destiny as soloists. No second wood-wind player is a satisfied man. He may have nothing but admiration for the first flute, oboe, or clarinet, as the case may be, but he knows that it is he who should occupy the principal position, and must often meditate upon the cruel truth that a player of your own instrument cannot be regarded as your friend until he is dead.

The harpist, like the cat, walks alone. Except when Wagner demands a group of harps, or when another modern composer is satisfied with two, the exponent of this ancient instrument makes a lonely, if picturesque, figure. In most orchestras, the harpist is feminine, which somehow seems as it should be, although in the Cockerill family both father and son were renowned performers – but so were the daughters. In the Goossens family, Marie and Sidonie were destined for this instrument, apparently from birth, but this was for the practical reason that members of the fair sex were not admitted into the orchestra in any other capacity. Since then the rule has been increasingly relaxed, and following the lead given by Sir Henry Wood (that giver of leads in the orchestral profession), women play in the B.B.C. Symphony Orchestra, the Hallé, some orchestras in America and on the Continent. At first, their activities were restricted to the string departments, but more recently they have widened their territory to include most wind departments, and even the percussion. In all these instances, equality of pay is the rule. The L.P.O. has so far held out against all such blandishments, the harpist always excepted, but whether they will continue to follow this narrow tradition is a secret of the future. Curiously enough, I have seldom heard orchestral men argue in favour of admitting women to their ranks, although administrators take a more sympathetic view. But the question must ultimately be seriously debated, and we can no longer be satisfied to accept the harpist as the single flower against the black and white background of the masculine orchestra.

The intermittent nature of the harpist's work, when the instrument may be left unattended on the platform for the greater portion of the programme, might lead the reader to suppose that this player considers herself – or himself – to be in the orchestra but not of it, but the truth is otherwise. John Cockerill was, at one time, a director of the L.S.O., while his sister, Winifred, no less than her colleagues of the Goossens family, identify themselves completely with the interests of the organizations to which they belong.

What do orchestral players do in their spare time? Do they spend all their leisure in perfecting the mastery of their instruments? Even the least enthusiastic musician has to devote a certain proportion of each free day to this activity, for music is a hard taskmaster, and after many years of close study of instrumental technique a player will feel dissatisfied and frustrated until he has performed his daily quota of practice. For string players, whose skill depends so much on the suppleness of their fingers, this is an obvious necessity, but wind players are no less punctilious. Horn players and those of the brass will spend some part of the morning after breakfast in satisfying their consciences and regaining their *embouchure*, and at any moment during the day may produce a mouthpiece from their pockets and curious *staccato* sounds from their lips.

There are certain players to whom music is the whole of life, whose devotion and constancy to the art allow them no sidelong glances at the manifold attractions of life; but they are rare, and, I think, fortunately so. The great majority follow other pursuits which supplement their activities and broaden their outlook as human beings. Politics interest only a small number, which has grown since the war has exposed to them their particular and insecure place in a changing social scheme. Purely intellectual studies do not find many followers, for the youth of those who are destined to become professional musicians is too much directed upon restricted lines to allow full development to the enquiring spirit. Nevertheless, I have met players with an extensive knowledge of oriental religions, who spoke foreign languages and studied the appropriate literature, who played chess with skill and enthusiasm, or who pored happily over a Latin author. These tastes are unusual, but anything which demands the use of sensitive hands and fingers finds a response among orchestral players, and a great deal of talent can be found in this direction.

A former trombone player of the B.B.C. Symphony Orchestra turned out some excellent stringed instruments, while a bass player and a viola player of the L.P.O. devote most of their limited spare time to the same pursuit. The music covers of the L.P.O. were at one time liberally adorned with malicious caricatures of conductors, and the *Philharmonic Post* is sometimes graced with photographs, the work of members of the Orchestra. Although the general reading of orchestral players is fairly wide, literary talent is rare, and most efforts at literary compositions betray a curious inhibition in the use of words.

Although most athletic pursuits are taboo to musicians, watchful as they must be of muscular strains and stresses, most orchestras boast a cricket team at one time or another. For a pleasure so highly contrasted with their work, as the sun on the close-cut pitch compared with the glare of lights on a concert platform, many players will risk injured fingers or a damaged lip. The more prudent administrator may regard such activities with misgivings, fearing the loss of a key player, but his warnings will be ignored when the fine days come, and when the break between a run of concerts provides the occasion for an orchestral test match.

From this it will be seen that music in the lives of orchestral players is only one of many talents, and goes to disprove the remark once made that 'any fool can play the fiddle.' On the other hand, musicians suffer under the handicap of having little contact with the outside world; they live, play, and travel together, often marrying musicians, with the result that a kind of intellectual in-breeding takes place, tending farther and farther away from reality. While music was a luxury profession this was to be expected, and could not be obviated, but when it has become one of the necessities of a civilized existence such a state of things will no longer be accepted. But for this the whole basis of the musician's life must be transformed, and a keen interest in the control of his own affairs should go far in this direction.

9 The Problem of the Concert Hall

This chapter, although bearing the same title as the
corresponding chapter of the original edition, has been entirely
rewritten in view of post-war developments.

THE prospect of developing symphony orchestras cannot be
separated from a survey of concert halls. This axiom
received little attention in the past when, with a few exceptions, halls were erected for a variety of purposes among
which concert giving was not included. The results have
been far from happy.

It is seldom fully realized how great a part the existence
of a concert hall has played in the development of musical
culture. A striking instance is that of the Concertgebouw
(concert building) in Amsterdam, which gave rise immediately after its erection to the formation of the permanent
Concertgebouw Orchestra. This magnificent body has done
almost as much for the reputation of Amsterdam as have the
city's famous canals. And the audiences there have a musical
taste much superior to that of many other greater cities.

The concert halls of Germany, most of them now, alas, in
ruins, held up the structure of musical tradition and enabled
German musical activity to lead Europe for a remarkable
period. Who, having taken part in a performance at the
Leipzig Gewandhaus, can have failed to feel what that
perfect hall represented, with its uninterrupted history of

Mendelssohn, Schumann, Brahms, Nikisch, and the others? It is not only the loss of certain players which, since the war, has brought down the standard of the Berlin Philharmonic, now condemned to play in one of the ugliest of cinemas. Is it not more likely the loss of the Philharmonie which, although no more beautiful than Berlin itself, had a quality of acoustics and general dignity that enlivened the spirit?

Nearer home, we can remember that the building of Queen's Hall led to the foundation of the Queen's Hall Orchestra and the Proms, and that a little more foresight from the builders and the financiers might have given us a permanent orchestra almost contemporary with that of Amsterdam.

Many other examples from countries all over the world would show that a fine hall may bring to life a fine orchestra and a fine public, while an unsatisfactory building will fail in both respects and remain no more than a monument to the failure of its architect.

London has had its object lessons on concert halls since the war-time destruction of Queen's Hall. To those who performed there, its disappearance is a continued regret, and its deceptive walls, standing only to hide the ruins within, serve only to advertise concerts held elsewhere. Those of us who were vitally concerned with concert giving on that tragic day of 1941 could hardly perceive what the effects of its destruction would be. And had we done so, we were powerless to react against the force of circumstances.

By these, we were driven to the Royal Albert Hall. A great deal has been written and spoken against this Victorian memorial, with its famous echo, its infamous draught, and its lack of comfort and intimacy. That it has served its purpose as a place where concerts could at least be held cannot be denied. But what it has done to the concert-going public of our greatest city has yet to be computed. That it enshrines some doctrines of a bygone age is beyond doubt, yet few people are aware that, in spite of an enormous and relentless charge for rental, almost a third of the effective seating is the property of private owners who are able to occupy – or to sell to another the right to occupy – seats for performances which have cost orchestral societies extravagant sums, but to which they as seatholders have contributed nothing. In more expansive moments, one may summon up some gratitude to those whose subscriptions made the building of the hall possible; but if this continued privilege to their heirs is difficult to comprehend in these days, what must we think when we learn that twentieth-century commercialism allows the privilege to be cornered, so that companies set up for the purpose may buy up seats and thus raise one more obstacle in the path of musical progress?

This anachronism will, no doubt, be corrected, but the effects of this gigantic arena on our musical public may take longer to pass. When we read the words of a critic, writing in 1950, who says:

... there can be little doubt that public concerts are already declining in importance and that an increasing number of music-lovers – and among them not the least discriminating – seek their musical pleasures from the radio and the gramophone.

we can assume two things: first, that most of his listening has been confined to the Royal Albert Hall, and that his general conclusions are therefore invalid, and secondly, that many other listeners, who have not even the professional duty to cover music elsewhere, have been driven away to the radio or gramophone.

Music demands an intimacy between listener and performer which is liable to be lost in any large hall, and can, indeed, only be presented by the fortune of good acoustics and the skill of the architect in creating a sense of unity in the audience. The Royal Albert Hall is the negation of both qualities; the members of its audiences have no relation to the orchestra, and little more to each other. There is no impact of the music upon the ears, no dramatic appeal within the normal limits of orchestral sound. Music is heard as if at second hand.

After a long period of such listening I went to Amsterdam for a performance of two Beethoven symphonies, the 5th and the Choral. For the first half hour I was shocked by this almost forgotten direct relationship with an orchestra. Here was the true orchestral sound, the aggressive quality of the trumpets and trombones, the persuasiveness of the strings growing to an emotional climax where the attack had an edge on it, while the other instruments stood out in their real character. I realized at once that all the young generation of concert-goers in London were being cheated; they were hearing a travesty of an orchestra and believing that there was no more to it. Little wonder that the modern gramophone recording provided more exciting listening.

It was for this reason, I am sure, that audiences in Kensington have dwindled steadily since the end of the war. I am not here subscribing to the opinion of the critic I have quoted, for elsewhere audiences have remained steady or grown. But it can be stated without fear of contradiction that there is no longer an audience in this hall for a programme seriously chosen. Those, for example, who wish to hear a less-known work will prefer to study it at home, sacrificing the invigorating companionship of a concert for the pleasure of hearing and imagining the direct contact with the music.

The success of the Proms following their removal from Queen's Hall to the Royal Albert Hall may be placed against my argument. It has certainly presented the statistician with the material for a study. Whereas, up to 1940, the Prom audience fitted comfortably into the smaller accommodation, it immediately occupied a similar proportion of the Royal Albert Hall as soon as the concerts were given there, and has gone on growing ever since until, in 1950, the greatest number was accommodated since the series was founded in 1895. Stated barely in this way, it does seem to refute my argument. But what a price has had to be paid! And not only for the Proms, but for all concerts where the main intention has been to avoid financial loss.

Year by year, the tone of the Proms has declined. This is not merely that new composers and new artists find less place than they did when Sir Henry Wood reigned over them. The attitude of the audience, jammed into a solid mass where the word 'promenade' has lost all meaning, becomes more and more akin to a jamboree. The affectionate bonds between audience and conductor, or audience and players, have hardened into a noisy, hysterical tradition which has little relation to the joy of music, or to the genuine curiosity of the student. And programmes have been scaled down to meet this uncritical demand.

Genuine appreciation of symphonic music has thus been almost killed in London, making it one of the most backward areas of our country. And Queen's Hall lies, a gaunt relic to the inability of organizations with clashing interests to find an agreement which will once more raise stone upon stone and restore the concert atmosphere of our youth.

If this picture of London's poverty is depressing, it need not always be so. Queen's Hall will, no doubt, be rebuilt sooner or later, although the present demands on essential materials threaten to postpone it to the Greek kalends. In the meantime, the Royal Festival Hall is growing daily as I write this at the beginning of 1951.

The London County Council had long nursed a plan for developing the south bank of the River Thames, and wartime destruction made its realization more urgent and practicable. It needed only the proposal of a Festival of Britain to bring it to life. A central feature was to be a concert hall; not necessarily designed to supersede Queen's

Hall, but to offer a needed amenity to the enormous population on the Waterloo side of the river. In the absence of a new Queen's Hall, it will have to serve the whole of London, and will become for a time the show-piece of England.

The requirements of concert-goers have never been thoroughly understood by architects in this country. It seems to have been thought that, provided the hall held the audience with some degree of comfort (and proper ventilation was always forgotten), no further amenities were needed. A buffet or two, so small and so badly served that only the most thirsty and energetic section of the audience could hope to obtain refreshment during even the longest interval, represented the limit of informal pleasure for listeners. In the hall itself, a high platform, often railed off, guaranteed complete separation between the performers and those who heard them.

Behind the scenes, a similar parsimony reigned, ensuring that the artists enjoyed few opportunities of relaxation, and none at all of preparation. Halls in many other countries were more intelligently designed. Fortunately, the group of architects employed by the L.C.C. had no intention of being bound by past English practice. They went abroad to see what had been done elsewhere. Furthermore, they guessed that musicians might have something useful to say on the detailed lay-out of a hall. One of their first actions was to invite advice from officials of the L.P.O., and in 1947 a detailed schedule concerning the entire concert building was drawn up. Practice rooms for individual players, rehearsal rooms for the choir, a replica of the platform in a soundproof room enabling two orchestras to rehearse simultaneously without interfering with each other, lockers for the players' possessions, and many other suggestions were put forward and adopted. Later, a questionnaire was circulated among members of the L.P.O. on platform arrangements, and much of the annoying awkwardness of other platforms was avoided.

The audience was not envisaged merely as a procession of people who paid at the box-office and eventually left through an exit leading straight into the street. In the hall itself, visibility and audibility were guaranteed to everyone, based on a design which avoided any arbitrary division between the orchestra and the audience. And then, the foyers. It was realized at once that some thought had to be given to the social, physical, and psychological aspects. Both before and after a concert it is pleasant to meet friends in comfortable surroundings, and to discuss what we are about to hear or, better still, what we have just heard. To leave a concert hall after a vital experience and fight for a seat in a bus or train, to jostle for a place in a crowded café, surrounded by people not blessed with the same experience, is to become aware of an anti-climax. One does not want to dive into the cold bath of everyday life quite so rapidly.

In the new hall there will be no reason for such a sudden transposition. Its site on the river could hardly be bettered, and this has been fully exploited in the pattern of cafés, restaurants, lounges, and corridors where the audience can fully savour its evening's entertainment. If the final building approximates to the architects' early vision, London will have a concert hall which may become the envy of Europe. There only remains the problem of creating a policy which will bring the hall to life. When this has been achieved, and it may well take much longer than the actual building, a new door will be opened on the brilliant opportunities of London's musical future, through which we shall see a planned pattern of concert-giving which will counteract the disastrous effects of the post-war years. Without such a policy, the hall may become, in spite of all its advantages, a gigantic white elephant. If I restrain myself from expecting too much it is because I know that the cause of music calls for something more than the petty place-seeking or the safe and cautious operations of functionaries to whom music represents a job like any other. Policy making will demand the same imaginative sweep which has carried the architects over the natural obstacles of the South Bank.

*

This more hopeful outlook in London must not be allowed to distract attention from the rest of the country. The concert hall which distinguished every self-respecting German town before the war has had no parallel here, and the comparison between musical standards is not without its connexion. Until just before World War II, few towns in England had halls where concerts could be given satisfactorily; even the best of them, like the Philharmonic Hall in Liverpool, were too small. The Free Trade Hall in Manchester and the Bristol Colston Hall were two of the most suitable, but both were destroyed before the end of the war. In Manchester an unexpected alternative was found at Belle Vue, a stadium of unencouraging aspect but which, treated as an arena with the orchestra in the centre, surrounded by serried ranks of concentrated listeners, creates a warm communal atmosphere and provides acoustic clarity. The reopening of the Free Trade Hall will present the Hallé Orchestra with new opportunities, and link it again with its famous tradition.

The Colston Hall, around which in the years immediately before its destruction an intelligent young audience was growing, is expected to be rebuilt by the time these words are printed. Unfortunately, the seating capacity, never too great, will be reduced and will confront visiting orchestras with added economic problems. These are common to most other halls in England and Wales. Scotland is better served in its main cities, and the Scottish National Orchestra has several strong bases from which to carry out its operations. Even where large halls are built in England it is rare to find that the architect has kept in mind the acoustical and other qualities which are essential in obtaining satisfactory orchestral performances. I may incur the wrath of the inhabitants of Sheffield, one of the most musical of provincial towns, if I repeat the criticism so often levelled at their City Hall by Sir Thomas Beecham; but here is an excellent hall with a platform so disposed that the orchestra must be spread out in such a way that without a telephone service between the conductor and some sections of the players no communication is possible. If, one day, the people of Sheffield wish to erect a monument in honour of Sir Thomas, their task will be easy. They have but to remove from the City Hall platform the two rampageous lions whose presence there is so unwelcome and embarrassing, and mount them sphinx-like upon the moors outside the town; a future Shelley will read from them, not 'the sneer of cold command', but the hearty commonsense of those who transported them.

Cinemas and Methodist Central Halls have offered the only platforms in many towns, but neither are normally available on Sundays, when audiences can most easily be attracted. Cinemas were most valuable during the war, but few proprietors are now prepared to sacrifice their regular profits for the uncertain speculation of symphony concerts. Such exceptions as the Davis Cinema of Croydon, where the music-loving family of this name welcomes musical performances, make it possible to bring an orchestra regularly to an area otherwise almost completely neglected. But, generally speaking, cinemas must be left out of a wide plan.

Central Halls have many practical faults, but a great number of towns rely exclusively upon them for all musical activities. At the period of their building, choral music was in its heyday, and orchestral concerts were still too rare for architectural consideration. Platforms, therefore, accommodate only a minimum number of players, and these ascend rapidly heavenwards up a steep rake which mixes violinists and viola players with bass instruments and percussion, to the extreme discomfort of all concerned. The conductor is fortunate if he can find the players he wants when the score indicates their entry. But atmosphere can nevertheless be created, and those who administer these halls help to bring a warmth to the proceedings often absent from more dignified buildings.

If we are to build the mass audiences which must be the aim of orchestral societies, the halls we hope to build must be acceptable to the people as their own halls. Should we fail in this, we shall offer them symphonic music in vain. Sir Cyril Fox, at one time director of the National Museum of Wales, once told me the following story: He was sitting by the desk at the entrance of the museum, the hall of which was decorated with a number of very fine statues and marbles. Two miners from one of the Welsh valleys pushed their way through the swing doors and paused for a moment to survey the works of art displayed before them. 'Looks like a bloody graveyard, Dai,' said one of them, and both turned on their heels and left the museum. This feeling that museums, concert halls, and civic buildings have not the warmth of life in them is a great danger to propaganda work on behalf of any of the arts; the public must be made to feel no less at home in the concert hall than in the music-hall or cinema; otherwise we shall continue to play to the converted or to those who, by an inversion of the same feeling, come to concerts because it is the thing to do. During the thirties several municipalities embarked on the daring course of building civic halls in which concerts could take place. Southampton, Wembley, Watford, Walthamstow, and Wolverhampton are among the more outstanding, and, although the enterprising councillors were assailed by nervous ratepayers, time – and the good fortune of surviving the war – have justified their courage. The attitude of present councillors varies considerably from town to town. In one, the hall might be called the 'ratepayers' joy', for the rents from dances, meetings, concerts, and other social activities are extremely profitable and are, in fact, judged by that very test. If culture is to cost money they will have none of it, and their citizens are forced to leave the district and travel in search of it. Such councillors were happy when, during the brief post-war boom, visiting orchestras fell over each other in their anxiety to profit from the prevailing enthusiasm. Warnings that such a wealth of music would fail were ignored, and to-day the result of such uncontrolled competition has left more than one town entirely bereft of symphony concerts.

Others, more wise and, I am glad to say, more numerous, were prepared to exercise a measure of control, allowing a fixed number of concerts each year at reasonable intervals, and now have steady audiences which benefit by the continuity of listening which is all-important. This belief in free competition in a pursuit which is essentially unprofitable has defeated several attempts at putting local concert-giving on a secure basis, but although Central Halls in some towns refuse to lose any bookings in the interest of planning, the general principles of better sense are becoming widely appreciated. Consequently some hundred centres are now enjoying regular concerts where, only ten years ago, nothing of the kind had ever been heard. The propaganda of the orchestras and of the Arts Council is having its effect.

We have seen that the future of the symphony orchestra in England is intimately bound up with the question of halls. There is no hope of putting our leading orchestras on their feet, and no hope of a genuine decentralization of musical opportunity until a circuit of halls runs through the country. The immediate prospect of such an achievement could hardly be less encouraging. The hopes which sustained our efforts since 1939 are again deferred, for private enterprise can no longer face the cost of such building, and municipal authorities, although given power by Parliament and desire by their citizens, cannot obtain the various permissions for straw to make the bricks.

This is not a cry of despair. If London, in the midst of our present crises, can realize its dream of a grand new hall, other towns will not let the achievement go unnoticed. The make-do of so many municipal experiments to-day is teaching us many lessons, and when sanity descends upon the world once more the knowledge will be put to good use. So much of our present economy is false. Our orchestras clutch desperately at the swinging trapeze, and municipal funds provide a net to break the fall. If the halls we are asking for were brought into existence, much of the need for such assistance would vanish. The public of our many cities, attracted by pride in their own halls, would sustain our organizations with a loyalty never yet discovered elsewhere.

10   *The Building of Programmes*

WHEN the guest enters the strange salon to which he has been invited, his first thought will be to find one familiar face which will serve as a *point d'appui* while he takes stock of his fellow guests, and as a *point de départ* for the making of new acquaintances. On sighting the friend he will feel at once at home, and will be prepared in a more tranquil frame of mind to scrutinize the other faces, and accept or reject them according to the impressions he receives. It may be that the friend whose presence a few moments ago gave him a sense of relief and comfort may prove a dull fellow, or the brilliance and wit of which he had in the past made such display may fail to scintillate against the genuine sparkle of the assembled company. Slowly, certain of the other guests will stand out from the throng, their personalities will impinge themselves upon his, and he will feel rather ashamed at having in a moment of weakness allowed himself to depend so much on such a second-rate creature.

At a popular concert given by the London Philharmonic Orchestra in Blackpool some years ago, the programme included, for rather obvious reasons, the *Rhapsody in Blue* of George Gershwin, a much publicized but trivial work which had acquired a wide reputation for reasons little connected with music. Popular fancy was attracted by the spectacle of the jazz musician turning his skilful attention towards symphonic music; a success similar in reverse order to that

of Ravel in *Boléro*, and occasioning a surprise rather analogous
to that aroused by the poetical achievements of W. H.
Davies, the tramp, of Robert Burns, the ploughman, or, on
a different plane, by the erstwhile bricklaying of Mr Winston
Churchill. One is reminded of Dr Johnson's comparison of
a woman's preaching to a dog walking on its hind legs:
'It is not done well, but you are surprised to find it done at
all.' The mixed audience of Blackpool, amused perhaps by
the incongruity of the item, filled the hall, which accommodated 4,000 people, only to find that the musical wit they
had so pleasurably anticipated proved small beer in the
august company beside which it was presented. The Fifth
Symphony of Beethoven secured the honours in no uncertain
fashion.

Many such considerations which may be called psychological have to be borne in mind when programmes are
being built to attract audiences unaccustomed to the study
of a list of musical works, and they will vary according to
the type of audience, the kind of hall, and even the town
concerned. While almost any audience which is more
generalized than a narrow coterie will object to any obvious
attempt at musical education, it will object no less to an
undisguised 'playing down', a sure sign of the musician's
contempt for his listeners. When a programme is designed
for an inexperienced audience it is important to provide it
with an introductory 'friend', the name of which they
recognize and which they have heard favourably discussed.
As the Blackpool incident shows, this work may cease to be
the primary attraction when compared with the other
items, and this may be an excellent thing; it is indeed the
first step in a musical education.

For any audience there are one or two composers who
never fail to satisfy. The outstanding example is Beethoven,
who, like Shakespeare, has something to offer to every man.
It is, indeed, this richness of appeal which is a proof of the

composer's greatness and universality, and the many levels
at which such music can be enjoyed is relevant to the whole
question of musical appreciation. Much has been written
and spoken on this subject, but much of it misses the mark
very widely. The first essential to the enjoyment of music is
just that and no more; the listener must enjoy himself when
he hears music. This sounds trite enough, but a little honest
avowal on the part of many concert-goers will give it greater
importance. Young people enjoy music wholeheartedly and
almost entirely from an emotional angle. They rarely have
either the training or the technical knowledge necessary for
a complete concentration on all that they are hearing, but
as a first stage the purely emotional response is no less
healthy than essential. It is a stage of musical innocence
which is much to be envied; like most innocence, it is soon
lost and is eternally regretted. The next step is a purely
intellectual one; the enquiring listener will cease to be
satisfied with standing outside the mysteries of the art, and
although he may play no instrument he will want to know
how music is made up and by what laws it is controlled and
guided. But here lies the greatest danger. From now onwards, he is not satisfied to listen and feel what the music
has to communicate; he begins to think. Not that I deprecate
thought about music or any other subject; God knows there
has been little enough of it among the majority of people,
but between feelings and thoughts on music there is an
antagonism and an antithesis which must be resolved. The
usual result of thinking about music, the most abstract of
all arts, is a denigration of its emotional possibilities, an
attempt to define and restrict it within arbitrary laws. This
attempt to explain the unexplainable, to sound the un-
fathomable depths of musical intuition, is apt to become
little more than mathematics. Those who are at this stage
must guard against preferences and prejudices which will
erect barriers between them and the music itself. They will

try to maintain an objectivity in their judgement which may rob them of the true meaning of what they are hearing; they will go to a performance with opinions ready made, and will struggle to maintain them against the ever-diminishing whisper of their earlier innocence.

The vast majority of regular pre-war concert-goers belonged to this class of listener, and they are a problem. Many critics can be found among them, and their grudging attitude is the programme builder's load of mischief. Not for them the unalloyed enjoyment of music for its own sake. A programme will never be taken simply for the pleasure it provides; each item will be judged by new, and often inadequate, standards with a fatal finality of opinion. When this is but a youthful priggishness there is little harm done, for there is still the time and vitality to struggle through to the third stage, where emotional pleasure and intellectual knowledge fuse into a synthesis which is the highest form of musical appreciation. This ideal balance of thought and feeling makes it possible to find the true value and meaning of a work, irrespective of its period and mode of expression.

To arrive at this final stage of musical appreciation demands, I think, no less genius in one way than the finest type of interpretative artist needs in another. It is far more than a question of musical knowledge or experience, and calls for the complete integration of the personality of the listener.

An example of the three stages I have referred to can be taken from the common type of reaction to the music of Beethoven, which in many ways is the touchstone in musical appreciation. Newcomers to symphonic music, with no specialized knowledge and no pretensions, are like the Blackpool audience mentioned above; Beethoven offers no difficulties to them, but provides a profound emotional experience. At the second stage the listener finds Beethoven rather trite and obvious; he looks for composers who display more orchestral brilliance, who break more rules and introduce more subtle harmonies, and whose works are beyond the comprehension of the common man. He is the person who has given up plain food, which is merely nourishing, and wanders round Soho for Chinese cooking, Hungarian wines, and other restoratives to a jaded palate. But if he is wise, he will treat these adventures on the fringe as a complementary experience, and sooner or later will return to the heart of things. In the music of Beethoven he will find all he sought, but now he will be able to appreciate the great simplicity of these masterworks with a heightened power. He has reached a higher plane of aesthetic enjoyment, and will set out on new adventures with no danger of losing himself.

With those who have reached this high point of development we need not concern ourselves. The programmes we are building are not for them. It is the newcomers and those who have a little and dangerous knowledge that we are planning to attract and please. And there is a serious division between them. Often enough, when a list of forthcoming programmes is submitted to concert-goers of a little experience, they consider the items with a deprecating smile.

'Are they still playing these old things over and over again?' they enquire superciliously. 'The number of times I've heard Beethoven 7 and the "Unfinished"! It's about time they were given a rest.'

Such critics overlook the very important fact that for many members of the audience the performances they are dismissing so lightly, far from being the nth performance of a hackneyed work, are the doorway to a new world of wonder and delight. They forget that everyone has to hear this or that work for the first time, and that what is tiresome to them may be an unforgettable experience for someone who is only just discovering the wealth and beauty of the orchestral treasury. In their superiority, these folk are apt to forget how much they owe to the works they treat so contemptuously. They do not realize, perhaps, that it is due to repeated hearings of this or that symphony that they are able and anxious to look for new worlds to conquer, and in refusing to grant others privileges they have enjoyed they are denying the principles of their own development.

This plea on behalf of the standard works of music must not be taken as an excuse for humdrum programme building, for an audience, like an individual, progresses steadily and rapidly if the means are provided. If modern Promenade audiences at the Royal Albert Hall were treated to the programmes originally offered to them by Sir Henry Wood fifty-odd years ago they would rightly jeer, or stay away. Although such an audience is constantly changing, it follows a definite line of development and, if rightly led, will give evidence of a steadily improving collective taste. But even the highest point of development at any time will not satisfy the most enlightened section of that audience, and those who compose it will look for something beyond the honest-to-God routine performances which are all that can be reasonably demanded for such a series of concerts. They will come to expect more subtlety and art both in interpretation and orchestral technique, and, having outgrown the Proms, may look back upon them with disdain, forgetting that their very power of deeper appreciation constitutes the finest compliment they can play to the inspired indefatigability of Sir Henry Wood.

So that those responsible for the designing of programmes must allow for the more advanced members of their audiences, while not forgetting to base their plans on the unassailable works of the greatest composers. This will save them from the fault of offering complete and indigestible programmes of modern works to any audience except one composed of specialists; it will also save them from devoting all their attentions to the three B's. The chronological path may profitably be followed, although not too rigidly, and it is important to demonstrate that modern composers – apart from experimentalists – do not create their works upon new foundations and principles, but carry those principles to a further stage of development. The greatest composers are those whose works do not lead to an artistic cul-de-sac, but open a new and wide road for exploration. The great artist may sum up an epoch, but does not close it; he will not fail to inaugurate a new one. So the generations of mankind pass on the torch of human culture.

The introduction of new or unfamiliar works creates many difficulties, particularly in the case of an orchestra which labours under the absurd necessity of having to make concerts 'pay for themselves'. In the past, the works of British composers have always been prejudiced by inadequate rehearsal and isolated performances. However progressive a musical organization may be, it is wrenched back into the rut by financial considerations, and its attitude to the encouragement of young composers is governed by these sordid details. An extra rehearsal will often mean the financial failure of a concert, and as a result the first performance of a work on which the reputation and future of the composer may depend is inadequately prepared. It is, then, not surprising that the public shows no anxiety to hear the composition again.

With frequent tours on the lines followed by the L.P.O. since the war, this difficulty can be overcome in a certain measure. Once a work has been prepared it can be performed at various provincial centres and will very soon become part of the orchestra's repertory.

If this is to be done, the orchestra concerned must first win the confidence of its audiences. A permanent conductor whose bona fides are beyond doubt is most important, for although large audiences will readily accept lesser-known works when a foreign visitor with a famous name presents them, this will only be an occasional advantage, and the high prices charged will keep away most of those we are aiming to bring along with us. The Hallé under Barbirolli, and the L.P.O. with Boult, are now more than ever able to take these risks with provincial audiences. In the main city of the orchestra, where concerts are given more frequently, the problem is a more difficult one. In Manchester, a steady audience is no doubt growing, but in London it would be self-deception to make this claim. The reasons behind the near impossibility of achieving this in our capital city are beyond the scope of this chapter, but it has to be admitted that a programme containing a major unfamiliar work will certainly be played before a sparse audience.

Outside London, the difficulty still exists, but to a lesser degree, and it often happens that many more people will hear an adventurous programme in a town of 200,000 inhabitants than in London with its ten millions. Music clubs play some part in this, for they gather in all the known music lovers in the town, and by means of lectures, gramophone recitals, and the social appeal of concert-going, provide a more steady audience. Yet, even so, the distressing fact remains that an orchestral society intent on doing its duty to the players and to music itself can only look upon such composers as Bruckner, Mahler, and any Frenchman or Englishman of the twentieth century, as a dire threat to its solvency. If this state of affairs were noticeable only in England, we might conclude that ours was not a musical country and leave it at that, but my own experience has shown that other countries of long musical traditions suffer from it similarly. Everywhere there is this natural tendency towards music that is already known, already accredited; everywhere there is this flight from composers of our own time. Unless some clear and honest thinking is done about the problem, we may well lose in the end the benefits of the progress which has been made in bringing music to the people.

In addition to the small audiences which are the fate of new works, there are other financial considerations to be taken into account. The introduction of new works brings with it one of the commercial sides of music-making. The composer, if he is still alive, or his immediate heirs, will not unnaturally expect to receive some compensation for his gifted labours. This is covered by a fee paid for the right of performance, and there is a Performing Right Society which deals with this aspect of the question, and guarantees the interests not only of the composer, but of the publisher, who may have hazarded a considerable sum of money in preparing an edition of a new orchestral work. The fees due to this Society, although no doubt justified, are an added argument against the production of any number of new compositions, for the appearance of the unknown piece in a programme is far from being an attraction in our present stage of musical development, and the double handicap may just force a decision against its inclusion. The hire of the musical material is also a heavy charge, and one of the obvious contradictions of our present system is shown when a house of music publishers will go to considerable lengths to persuade an orchestral organization to perform a new work, and then send in an account which is likely to cure the organization of any desire to repeat the experience. This is the reverse of the 'song-plugging' methods about which so much has been said and which, if we are to believe it all, provides a solid encouragement to musicians of a certain type to sponsor new compositions.

In these days of extreme uncertainty, any sensible organization will have its eyes turned more to the future than upon the obsession of present quotidian details, and we can therefore afford to ignore material difficulties and concentrate upon the task of attracting large audiences by well-balanced programmes. The aesthetics of programme-building need not concern us unduly; that is a question for the specialist. What we must do and continue to do is to remember that every audience includes many of those to whom a symphony concert is a complete novelty, and who must not be allowed to go away unsatisfied and disappointed. Those whose experience of concerts has given them a healthy curiosity for more advanced movements in music must not be forgotten, and the perfect programme will be one which achieves the impossibility of pleasing everybody.

II *Interlude II*
On Audiences in General

I ONCE knew a young composer who, as soon as he had rid himself of the irritant creative urge by writing a work, was content to add the title of the composition to his list of works, place the manuscript in a drawer on top of a pile of its predecessors, and forget all about it while waiting for the Muse to call on him again.

I think we may safely put him down as an exception. Almost all creative artists, and certainly all executants, find an audience an essential part of their life. Even while writing or preparing for the performance of a work, an imaginary audience exists in the background of their mind; although their own artistic standards may be the final arbiter of their work, listeners are needed to ratify those standards. This is why broadcasting is such deadly work for any sensitive musician; the unfeeling and unobtrusive microphone is no substitute for a living group of people, and while a single speaker may have some conception of the listeners who are following his words – and perhaps the telephone has prepared him for that – the musician, especially if he is playing in a concerted body, will miss the reaction of an audience which is such a valuable contribution to the performance. The case of Sir Thomas Beecham provides a striking instance of the truth of this remark. When he is rehearsing with the orchestra alone he will go through the work to be prepared with an apparent lack of enthusiasm, sometimes in a haphazard fashion; but place *one* listener in the body of the hall, and the atmosphere changes at once. The rehearsal suddenly becomes interesting, subtle effects are obtained, and the sparkle of his wit flashes like electricity.

Even the ordinary music-lover will gain something from being one of a number of people all concentrating, even subjectively, along the same lines. Here again the wireless suffers from a comparison with the concert hall. Listening to a broadcast concert when your wife is knitting and your daughter preparing her homework may be a friendly and charming occupation, but in addition to the fact that your attention will inevitably be distracted by the clicking of needles or the scratching of the pen – even when your domestic companions do not count stitches aloud or ask pertinent or tactless questions about long-forgotten problems – you will miss the positive presence of other music-lovers which deepens and, in a sense, justifies your concentration.

So we may accept an audience as a body of people who, in addition to being moved by the music, have it in their power to affect the performance of that music by their effect on the artists themselves. The relationship between such actions and reactions could probably be investigated by a more profound brain than mine, but the audience itself is, for the moment, my main consideration.

We are inclined to take an audience as being a static body, a mass which is always unified and turned in a certain direction. This is wrong. A group of people does not become an audience *proprement dit* until the music has got to work upon its individual sensibilities and moulded it into a collective body. Those folk who sit and admire or criticize the dresses of others, those who go through the programme and in a loud voice give incredibly false biographical details of the star performers, or those who are taking a last look at certain interesting points in the score before the performance begins, are not yet part of an audience. When the applause greets the entry of the musicians, the audience takes its first steps towards having an existence *per se*, and the strength of its cohesion will depend then on the power of the music, and even more, it must be regretfully admitted, on the power of the performers, to weld the numerous different personalities and temperaments into a unanimous whole. During the interval there will be a tendency to break away, and if the appeal of the music has been slight the sense of being one of a group will be lost to the individual. No one will have the feeling that he has a right to speak to anyone he meets in the corridors of the refreshment room, to take it for granted that his fellow-listener has been through the same emotional experience as himself. If an accident occurs in the street, the same emotions of fear, pity, and relief are common to all members of the crowd which gathers round, and a man will speak to his neighbour without the usual diffidence. In a concert hall the experience is similar, although more complex and on a higher plane. Thus, when the performance is really fine, when the sincerity of the conductor and artists is only equalled by the greatness of the music, the audience will cease to be a collection of varying human beings, and will become one indistinguishable whole. Even the critics will lose their customary objectivity and themselves in the general response.

Audiences capable of exercising genuine discrimination are very rare, and in any discussion of audiences the question of applause has to be faced. There are, of course, two points of view; that of the member of an audience, who might have said all I have written up to this point, and that of the artist to whom the applause is offered. The second point of view may profitably be sub-divided into the soloist and the orchestral player, and I venture to place more value on the opinions of the latter, who does not merely see the audience as he comes on, and is conscious of its applause ringing in his ears as he goes off, but also has the opportunity of sitting and watching the audience, if he has a mind to, go through the whole gamut of its feelings. He will notice some curious things.

Applause is largely imitative, and has a strange power of auto-excitement. With similar audiences, results will differ. The faithful ones who gather at the Royal Albert Hall from July to September have built up a tradition – one might almost say a *habit* – of applause. The precise moment following the conclusion of a work will be met by a sudden, full-strength burst of clapping, and although these audiences may not be classed among the most discriminating, the length of the applause and the amount of extraneous noise brought in to add strength may be taken as indicating the depth of appreciation felt by these enthusiasts, if not solely for the music, at least for the popular personalities who have presented it.

An opera audience, on the other hand, although often composed of many members of the one already spoken of, begins its applause more half-heartedly, often enough at the last note sung rather than the last orchestral chord of the work, a misguided enthusiasm which has often called down the wrath of the gods and Sir Thomas Beecham upon them. On more than one occasion, this conductor has taken it sufficiently to heart to repeat the last few bars of the orchestral score when his loudly expressed opinion of their philistinism, or the continued outstretching of his baton, has withered the unfortunate gatecrashers into silence. The full vociferocity of the opera-goer is reserved for the appearance of the solo singers in front of the curtain, and then it grows and grows – or so I believe, for most orchestral players, having a lower opinion of these stars, and having, in any case, seen and heard them in their more relaxed moments, find it difficult to work up enough enthusiasm to spend the valuable interval in star-gazing.

On Audiences in General

The tradition of applause in the opera house is a mystery which the experience of several years' regular opera attendance is insufficient to solve. *Parsifal* must, according to the best standards, be received in dead silence, and any attempt to express one's appreciation in the usual manner is rapidly hissed and murmured into nothingness. I once heard a courageous and convinced applauder continue in spite of these audible hints. He had my deepest sympathy, for if, as some psychologists say, applause is a necessary outlet for pent-up feelings, surely they never needed more relief than at the end of this pseudo-sacred service. After all, *Parsifal* takes place in a theatre, and is no mystery play.

Then there are the Italian operas, where the whole continuity of the work may be interrupted at a given point – usually indicated by an overheld top note of the tenor or soprano – and followed by an encore of the aria which has aroused the audience to this pitch of enthusiasm. If the character represented by the popular singer is thus made to die twice, it is little matter. The plot has been forgotten for the time being. In the earlier operas, where each number was complete in itself, and a short break was made before the next, there was, it is true, a certain excuse for such behaviour, but in more modern works, where the composer has been at pains to write music which carried the story right through, it is little better than vandalism, although to hope to correct it at this time of day is sheer tilting at windmills.

To go back for a moment to the concert hall, I would mention the tragic case of Weber's *Invitation to the Waltz*. This, as everyone should know, opens with an introduction in which the solo cello figures. This is followed by the waltz proper, at the end of which the cello resumes the solo and the composition ends as quietly as it began. I may have been unfortunate in my experience, but I cannot remember a performance in the theatre or the concert hall which has not been ruined by premature applause at the end of the waltz. As a result, the conductor must either wait for the misguided applauders to discover their mistake, or the first two or three bars of the cello solo are inaudible. In either case, the atmosphere of the piece is ruined. Weber was, of course, largely to blame for this contretemps. The waltz ends on a full cadence, with a feeling of finality which few listeners can resist. Had he left an air of expectancy before beginning the coda there would have been no trouble, but even so, it is a continual occasion for surprise that audiences have not yet become prepared for the anti-climax of this work, especially as most programmes explain the simple story which it is supposed to illustrate.

During a concert at one of our leading public schools, I was struck by the curious way in which the applause, which had been very full-blooded, came to an abrupt conclusion instead of petering out in the usual way. It was as if some sort of cheer-leader had been present in the hall, indicating when the applause had gone on long enough. This was made more striking still when, in the course of a concert tour of Germany, the same phenomenon was remarked in more than one town. The reader may ponder the problem of whether the discipline of everyday life has its concomitant in the concert hall. But the German audiences had a charming habit of crowding round the platform at the end of the performance, which is a more pleasant way of showing appreciation than any other.

We are often told by enthusiasts of the ballet that the great attraction of this form of entertainment is that it is a combination of so many arts. One can only suspect that these people are deceiving themselves. The only art to which they do, and perhaps even can, give their undivided attention is that of the dance. The *décor* has a secondary appeal, and the music comes a bad third. Few, if any, brains are able to be so divided that they are capable of using several faculties in a highly sensitive manner at one and the same time. Even critics will pass execrable performances on the part of the orchestra with little or no comment, suggesting that their usually intense critical attitude to music was weakened by other attractions. It may be suggested in their favour that they are being kind to musicians who have to grind out music while conscious of its secondary importance. Be that as it may, the manner in which a ballet audience will applaud a scene or a dance, or the entry of a favourite ballerina, is disconcerting to a musician at any time, but more so since Fokine, Massine, and others have used serious symphonic works as a foundation for their choreography.

These remarks on the subject of audiences and applause may have seemed rather unkind, more critical than complimentary, but much might have been said of well-behaved audiences who, while not lacking enthusiasm, are sensitive enough to know when and where to relieve their emotions and display their appreciation. The source of the trouble really arises in the fact of applause. To applaud or not to applaud has often been discussed, but since applause is such a well-established fact, and one which even the influence of Bayreuth cannot always restrain, any such discussion is purely academic. What would be more useful would be to recognize that if appreciation may legitimately be shown by clapping, the lack of it, or more positive disapproval, might be no less justly displayed. Some time ago, an enlightened member of one audience showed his distaste for what he had heard in no uncertain manner. He seems to have been reproved by all and sundry. I should like to see a medal struck in his honour, and a society of courageous music-lovers formed who would not hesitate to demonstrate exactly their reactions to certain music and certain performances. There can surely be nothing said in favour of applause which cannot also be put forward on behalf of any expression of displeasure. At least, it would give a value to applause which it does not now possess, and might make it at length possible to exercise criticism in the concert hall. A unanimous audience might subsequently be more difficult to attain, but the artist who achieved it would recognize his triumph.

12 *Music Betrayed*

IT is often thought that music, in common with other cultural forms, has maintained an existence unaffected by the change and progress of social conditions. We are told again and again that it is quite separate from life, and too abstract even to rub shoulders with all that is going on around it. This is far from being true, and although the interrelation of society and the art of composition cannot be traced without a great amount of historical research, the connexion between the practice of music and the trend of social life can much more easily be seen.

By the time music had become a conscious art it was already in the service of the Church, and both its forms and practical activities were designed to meet the needs of religious ceremonies. Almost every musician of note during the sixteenth century worked for an ecclesiastical patron who, later, shared with enlightened members of the aristocracy the honourable task of fostering the art of music. Palestrina in Rome, Orlando di Lasso in Munich, Weelkes at Chichester Cathedral, and at the Chapel Royal a long succession of musicians headed by Tallis and Byrd devoted most of their labours to the writing of Church music and to the training of choirs.

After the Reformation and towards the end of the sixteenth century many musicians in England turned their attention to instrumental music, in which direction the even more profitable help of the aristocracy was to be obtained. This change of direction was due, not only to a desire to escape from the cramping effect of the religious development upon musical composition, but also to the easier communications which began to be available between England and the continent, where freer artistic expression was still possible. It was, indeed, a striking example of the effect which political, economic, and religious forces can have upon both the organization and the content of music.

During the following century, music-making rapidly became more highly developed, as with skilful craftsmanship orchestral instruments reached a higher standard of perfection. In England, Charles II had his band of twenty-four fiddlers at the Chapel Royal, and Purcell followed the many musicians who owed their excellent training to this establishment. In France, Lully was flourishing under the munificence of Louis XIV, and later, Couperin and Rameau, and Scarlatti in Italy, were enabled by court or ecclesiastical patronage to develop their art. Very few of these magnificent benefactors were able to realize what treasures they were helping to create for posterity. The display of wealth and luxury was symptomatic of an age which considered that rank and dignity could only be sustained by ostentatious and lavish expense. That period lives on in the even more pathetic figure of the modern plutocrat of the first generation, who, from a similar motive, decorates his walls with modern paintings of which he understands little or nothing. Artists knew how to turn such naïve generosity to good account, and the history of music would have presented a different story without it.

Handel, in Germany, was made chief musician to the Elector of Hanover and when he came to England generous pensions from Queen Anne and George I enabled him to produce his greatest works. While his contemporary, Bach, was devoting all his tremendous energies to the service of the Church, Handel used the advantages of his position to write for a larger and more profitable public, thus opening the way for future developments.

It can be said that during these two centuries the chief opportunities for a musician to earn a living in England were by service in a private family, a position as a cathedral organist, or by service in the Chapel Royal. In other European countries conditions were very similar, and it will be seen that this system of patronage had a beneficial effect on the progress of musical art, which at that time was going through a period of rapid growth and sorely needed the support of people with money, power, and culture; but although this support was continued throughout the eighteenth and nineteenth centuries, a new spirit was soon to make itself felt. Haydn was perhaps the last of the great musicians who were content to exchange an almost complete servitude for an assured position in which they could work. As Hadow says: 'The relation implied in this patronage was, for the most part, frankly that of master and servant. As a rule, genius sat below the salt, and wore a livery like the butler or the footman. No doubt, the master was often genial and kindly, no doubt the gap was often lessened by the prevalent simplicity of manners; but the system in general was not well qualified to raise the dignity of art or to increase the self-respect of the artist.'

While it is true that Mozart, Beethoven, and many of their successors owed their early training and opportunities to generous patrons, the individual artist began to realize his own dignity, and to chafe under the restrictions imposed by his benefactors. Mozart was one of the first to display this spirit of independence. There is the famous story of his relations with the Archbishop Hieronymus, his patron for a long period, who treated him as a domestic servant and abused him freely. We are told that Mozart's appointment with the Archbishop was ended by a violent scene, after which the composer was kicked out of the room. While we may understand the high dignitary's outraged vanity and sense of importance, we can have nothing but sympathy and admiration for Mozart who, with no support but the faith in his own genius, appears to have had a quick and pertinent retort ready in answer to the abuse of his not very aristocratic patron. Although Beethoven dedicated many of his works to one or other of his benefactors, he had few doubts about his own importance as an artist in relation to their exalted status. It was he who refused to raise his hat to a personage of high rank, an action which Goethe, who was with him, did not fail to perform.

By the nineteenth century, conditions had changed in such a way that musicians were able to obtain a far greater measure of independence. Public concerts, easier travelling, opera houses, and the publishing of music offered them more and more possibilities of commercial success. With the growth of the middle class, many musicians were assured by birth of the means of an adequate education and, although Germany and the princely patrons were still in evidence, their activities had ceased to be entirely beneficial or necessary. Direct patronage had only been given to composers and solo artists, but orchestral players, whose work depended on assistance from one source or another, also shared their appreciation of the artist's dignity and his need for independence. In addition, for example, to the rebellion which founded the L.S.O., musicians formed themselves into protective societies, among which the Musicians' Union and the Incorporated Society of Musicians, were prominent. The history of their struggles to save the rather guileless musicians from the exploitation of the more commercial section of the profession would make exciting reading. But this was to come later.

It may be said that the system of individual patronage in

Germany, where it lasted longest and had the greatest influence, came to an end with Liszt in Weimar. Although he did not need the financial aid of the Duke of Weimar, Liszt was able to use the privileged position assured him by the Court to help the advance of the 'Music of the Future' in a magnificent and far-sighted manner. From this period onwards, in spite of King Ludwig's timely aid to Wagner, Court interest became a stumbling-block in the path of musical progress. This was shown when performances of Wagner operas were prevented by the powerful King of Saxony when that composer's activities in revolutionary politics had displeased him.

In his autobiography, *Buffets and Rewards*, Weingartner gave a vivid description of the way in which the once-beneficial system of Court patronage had become a network of intrigues which made the progress of sincere art almost impossible. But, in the meantime, much good had been achieved, and its effect has lasted until the present day. For as long as we can remember, it has been a commonplace that the English are an unmusical race, while the Germans oozed music at every pore. Whether there can be found ethnological grounds for such belief I do not know, but I prefer to attribute German predominance in the musical world very largely to the consistent help given to the art by those able to dispense it. In the field of composition, the number of musical organizations in Germany offered almost unlimited scope for young composers who, in England, would have wasted their sweetness on the desert air of their study. Our dearth of native conductors provides another sad comparison with Germany, where any musician with more than a ha'porth of talent could gain all the essential experience in an opera-house or concert-hall of a provincial town. The effect on audiences would be no less marked, and whereas in England a symphony concert is still regarded as a highbrow entertainment, in Germany it rapidly became a normal adjunct of life. Many of us have known young Germans or Austrians who, though ignorant of all musical theory and technique, could recognize and sing the subjects of all the standard symphonies and, what is more, discuss their form and structure in a highly intelligent manner.

In England, however, the development of music followed different lines and led to frustration. Private patronage declined very early and this, allied to the following of Handel's example of playing to the public, resulted in a deplorable decline of artistic standards. While the Chapel Royal continued its educational work, the accusation that all English musicians were Church organists was largely true to the end of the nineteenth century. Apart from the music with a definitely popular appeal which, in view of the existing lack of musical education, was inevitably bad, Church music was the only field which offered material returns.

This early decline of patronage was a sad blow for English music, coming as it did before any other demand made it possible for musicians to devote themselves to the progress of their art. As a result, almost every prominent musician in Victorian England was either imported or was a member of the middle class, having had opportunities of education and travel denied to the majority. This fatal separation from the people, the life-blood of society, was responsible for the stagnation of English music, as any comparison with conditions in Germany and France will show. Even in a symphony orchestra it was unusual to find an English musician in any prominent position, although the few who were distinguished soon began to assert themselves and their claims for recognition. In connexion with the Royal Philharmonic Society, Mr Stanley announced that 'he had found a fine song of Mercadante's, with a cello obbligato for Signor Pezze; Mr Walter Pettit protested that neither Signor Pezze nor anyone else should be allowed to usurp his post of leading violoncellist.' But many years were to pass before the English player was to establish himself, and it is necessary to go no farther back than the beginning of the Promenade Concerts to find an orchestra largely composed of foreign musicians. France, Belgium, and Germany supplied their quota, and among our best players to-day can be found the completely anglicized descendants of such musicians as Adolf Borsdorf and Eugène Goossens. It says much for Sir Henry Wood's perseverance and encouragement that, even before World War II, English musicians began to exercise their national heritage.

With the twentieth century, music in England has displayed more vigour, but its effects have been restricted to London and a few large towns, whose wealth and populations attract the best talent of the whole country, and the outstanding world musicians whose visits stimulate native efforts. The consequent depletion of large areas of all professional musical activities, with its denial of culture to the ordinary man, is a natural corollary of our decadent and over-centralized way of life. It is also the natural result of our continued neglect of music, and of our persistent refusal to give it a place in our public life. Whereas in so many other countries there has been a long and unbroken tradition of patronage, from the religious authorities to the princes, from them to kings, and by easy stages to municipalities and government departments, we have almost no precedent to follow. For two or three centuries the art of music in England has been left to the haphazard care of private individuals, whose efforts have been praiseworthy but not far-reaching, and whose artistic ambitions have always been doomed to ultimate failure, however glorious their personal careers may have been.

To all patronage, there must be a succession. In the heyday of princes and archbishops, the certainty of heredity in one case, and the laying on of hands in the other, established a continuity and guaranteed that whatever seed they sowed would be given time to come to fruition. In modern society, no man of wealth can be assured of the safety or certainty of his position, and it does not follow that his descendants will share his cultured interests. The only body of society which can be relied upon as constant and unchanging is the mass of people who provide audiences for the symphony orchestra. It is to them we must look for the future of music in general, and of the symphony orchestra in particular.

What form their patronage will take is a question which can only be answered by future social developments. At present it may become effective through the B.B.C., through municipalities, through Government departments, through existing trusts or philanthropic bodies, or direct to the musical organization itself. Or some quite new form, such as the organization of the whole musical profession as a many-sided industry, may answer the needs of those sections which are economically unsuccessful.

However this may be, it is quite clear from past experience that whatever assistance may be given to music, it will have to be justified in advance. Little or nothing will be forthcoming for the encouragement of musical activities; a much greater and wider public must first be won. It is this organization of the public which should be an important preoccupation of those responsible for creating and presenting music; when it has been achieved, we may possibly hope that the fact will be duly noted by those responsible for dispensing the national wealth, and that music will no longer be left to the vagaries of private charity and public appeals.

13 *Interlude III*
Gramophone Records

HAD Hector Berlioz been born a century later he might well have had the tortures of the gramophone recording studio in mind when he composed the *Marche au Supplice* as the fourth movement of his *Symphonie Fantastique*. The mental agonies of his 'artist' could not easily have surpassed those of the unfortunate musician (envied nevertheless by all his colleagues) who has to record upon wax the impression of his playing. To the listeners who hear only the smooth and flawless reproduction, there is little evidence of how such perfection has been achieved. They may wonder sometimes when, in the concert-hall, they hear doubtful intonation, imperfect tone, and unsteady ensemble, why such evidences of human weakness are so seldom noticeable on the machine-made record. It is just this clash between the machine and the human element which disturbs the musician taking part in gramophone recording. He knows that his work will not be listened to casually and that the effect of faults and imperfections will make more than the fleeting impression of the concert hall, for the gramophone has done much to rob music of its evanescent quality. We do not have to rely upon our memories to recall the details of such and such a performance of a favourite work; it is waiting for us 'on tap', and the familiarity with a certain set of records will reveal many hitherto unsuspected things including the slightest divergence from the truth on the part of the performer. And this is the bogey in the recording musician's nightmare.

To the soloist who has, as it were, only himself to blame, the business is not unduly complicated. Although the personal responsibility is greater he can rest assured that when his part is satisfactorily played and reproduced the record will take his name decently down to posterity. Even so, he must make many test records and spoil a good deal of wax before he and the experts agree that the reproduction has reached as near perfection as possible. He must be prepared to play four-minute selections of the work over and over again, forgetting for once the continuous form of the music in his endeavour to produce a version so free from blemish that the repeated concentration of the most critical gramophile will not discover the fact that the performer is human after all. Having left the studio feeling that all is well with the world, he may find himself summoned back a few weeks later to remake a record which, for one reason or another, falls short of the standard set by the remainder of the series. This section must then be repeated many times more, and pitch and tempo must be in keeping with that of the part which has already passed muster; the soloist must not share the temperamental uncertainty of Chopin, of whom it was said that he never played the same piece in the same way twice in succession. On this occasion, the section must be played precisely as before – only more so! There is a peculiar satisfaction in hearing a recording of one's own playing, a privilege denied to all those great artists who lived before the twentieth century, but in addition to this satisfaction, fame, finance, and the beckoning finger of posterity are needed to tempt the artist into the recording studio.

When a symphony orchestra is introduced into the studio the plot thickens, for here the possibilities of casual errors and a lack of unanimity are increased a hundredfold. The recording of concertos presents numerous difficulties, for the three points of view of the soloist, conductor, and orchestra will not immediately coincide. When the soloist is Jascha Heifetz there is little to worry about – the gramophone was made for him. It is safe to say that no human being has ever approached more nearly to the clean-cut accuracy of the machine than this violinist, and to watch him during a recording session is a fascinating experience. Here is the twentieth century worship of technique personified!

I remember a morning spent recording the Sibelius Concerto with Heifetz, Sir Thomas Beecham, and the London Philharmonic Orchestra. It was taken for granted that he knew the work inside out, the details of the orchestral parts no less certainly than his own, but it was amazing to hear him playing the same difficult technical passages time after time without the slightest deviation from the inhuman perfection of the first attempt. One particular phrase in up and down bow *staccato* stands out in my memory; one heard it, but still failed to believe that such an easy mastery of the instrument was possible. And when at last the tiresome business was finished he was entirely un- perturbed, while the conductor and the members of the orchestra were physically and mentally exhausted. But Heifetz is an exception who, had he lived like Paganini in a more superstitious age, would have had to satisfy his listeners that he had not sold himself to the devil. When I was once discussing his complete self-possession and lack of temperament with Lionel Tertis, he remarked: 'Oh, yes! We should all be as calm as that if we had half his technique.' But that is only half the story.

Fritz Kreisler, who not long before the war made new recordings of the Brahms and Beethoven Concertos with the L.P.O., has not based his reputation on such a devilish virtuosity, and it is not to be expected that a violinist with such warmth of nature, such intensity and sincerity of interpretation, could put a similar bold front upon his encounters with the recording microphone. His refusal to broadcast may be based on the same consideration. The continual repetitions appear to 'rattle' him; little mistakes creep in, intonation suffers, and one wonders for a moment what has happened. Is Kreisler growing old, and has he lost the skill and mastery of his fabulous youth? Such questionings come only as flashes and are immediately dispelled as the *cadenza* is reached, when, freed from the ties of conductor, orchestra, and time, Kreisler re-establishes himself as the unchallenged master of the violin and sails away into the innermost realms of beauty, while the musicians of the orchestra sit spellbound, as if the accompanying of the world's greatest soloists was not an everyday experience.

Other soloists become fidgety under the strain of pro-longed sessions, and this shows itself in different ways. Egon Petri, that sound musician and experienced recorder, was normally calm, patient, and good-humoured, but he rapidly became vexed with real or imagined shortcomings in his own playing, and he would discuss them impatiently with the players sitting near him. Artur Schnabel, on the other hand, allowed himself no such misgivings and frequently addressed himself to the orchestra without reference to the conductor, explaining how he wished this or that phrase to be accom-panied. But at one recording when a certain technical passage worried him, and the conductor, George Szell, counselled him not to be nervous, his forcible disclaimer, 'I'm not *nervous*,' made one wonder whether he too, in spite of a tremendous force of character, was not suffering from a fear of the all-too-truthful wax.

The symphony orchestra, alone in the studio, presents many problems. The seating of the musicians and their relation to the microphone usually discovers some disagree-ment as certain players find themselves in different positions from those occupied in the concert hall, with a corresponding difference in ensemble relations. As a session normally lasts for three hours there is little time to spare for the satisfaction of personal preference, and the orchestra soon has to settle down to the business of recording. A first period is usually spent in rehearsing the work to be recorded, and while this is going on studio attendants play with the microphones until the balance of instrumental power satisfies the listeners of the musical staff in their windowed cubby-hole at the end of the studio. If the music has not yet been cut into such lengths as can be taken by the single side of a record, stop watches become busy and consultations are held to decide at which point in the music the break is to be made. As soon as the parts have been marked accordingly these sections will be tried over, a test record being made, partly as a check on the precise length of the section chosen, and partly for balance and tone-quality. Where the selected ending for any particular side follows the logic of the music little difficulty will arise, but when the piece of music is such that an arbitrary decision has to be made one may safely wager 100 to 1 that a player whose thoughts are wandering (the mortal sin in any orchestra) will forget to stop playing at the chosen bar. When this occurs in making a test record the self-conscious trailing off will cause as much amusement as the annoyance which greets a similar exhibition of careless-ness during a master recording, when the whole orchestra will express disgust at the waste of so much meticulous work by mere thoughtlessness. Many of the most perfect record-ings have been denied the public by such a slip. But there are other causes. When the L.P.O. had spent a considerable time on the Slow Movement of the Second Symphony of Beethoven, perfecting the difficult passage for the horns, a superb performance was at last secured. Sir Thomas Beecham, relieved and pleased with a job well done and ignoring the warning red light which is only extinguished when the microphone is dead, exclaimed audibly and with evident satisfaction, 'Very good, gentlemen!' Although the archives of the gramophone company were enriched for posterity, the record had to be made again, with more tears and sweat.

There are times when nothing goes right. A chair slides with a hollow groan, a string breaks, a horn cracks a simple note, or a technical hitch on the engineering side will interrupt the proceedings.

'More money off the dividends,' mutters a player as a further effort fails, and a suppressed murmur greets the discordant sound of the buzzer which cancels out a last attempt. When the conductor is wise he will sense the atmosphere of nervous irritation and will send the players off to tea. This is a time-honoured institution at gramophone sessions, and after the hasty dash to the tea-room, and the leisurely return, progress will be more speedy.

*

The relation between the orchestral player and the gramophone companies has never been an easy one. In the early days there was a mistaken impression, which has nevertheless persisted in connexion with broadcasting and television, that the recording of music would act against the interests of musicians, and that, once it had become possible to listen comfortably at home, members of the public would no longer be persuaded to come to the concert hall. This has been proved false, and there is no doubt that the gramophone shares with the wireless set the honour of having introduced many people to music and led them by easy stages to live performances.

Although a serious proportion of the activities of the different gramophone companies has been devoted to the recording of jazz and music of the light and popular variety, certain pages of their catalogues have always been designed to please the serious music lover. This was true pioneer work for music, and at first preceded the public demand. Before long, however, public taste caught up, and the sale of records of this type must have represented a steady proportion of the companies' incomes.

The enthusiasm which is the driving force of all pioneer work is difficult to maintain; it is so much easier to follow public taste than to lead it, and gramophone companies have vacillated in their policy, cutting down serious recordings whenever the market tended to weaken. They argue, and in a commercial society no one will blame them, that the overhead expense of taking an orchestra and conductor into a studio makes profit slow to come by, and since the war this cost has increased so much that a word may be said by way of explanation.

When recording first reached the stage of perfection which made symphonic performances a practical proposition, musicians were unable to realize the implications of the position which faced them. A performance was a performance to them, irrespective of whether it took place in the concert hall or the gramophone studio; they did not appreciate the fact that a recorded performance once made was there, if not for all time, at least for many years, and that it could be presented to audiences exceeding by millions the number normally approached in a concert hall. A lack of vision, and a belief that 'a bird in the hand is worth two in the bush' persuaded players to accept conditions offered to them, although these were patently in favour of those who held the master records and copyrights. Once a record had been made and published, it might sell by the hundred thousand, but this meant nothing to the orchestral player, who received no royalties for his major part in the finished article.

The effect of this, and its full meaning, was brought home to me as a vivid reality early in the war. As I have recounted in a previous chapter of this book, the London

Philharmonic Orchestra was left high and dry for several weeks at the end of the summer of 1939. When the war broke out the members of the Orchestra had neither played nor earned fees for a considerable time; they sat at home, waiting in vain for the call to come, seeing their world in ruins at their feet. Some who had not seen the trend of events, or who fondly hoped that in any case such a famous organization as the L.P.O. would not be allowed to collapse, had made no preparations for this eventuality and were hard pressed to meet their various commitments. It was therefore with a sense of one of life's little ironies that they heard the B.B.C. announcer introduce a programme of records which they had made some months earlier. The records were still earning money to which they had no claim; they heard the ghosts of their former selves held up for public approval and enjoyment, while they, whose skill and art had gone to the making of the records, sat there neglected and forgotten.

Efforts to rectify this unsatisfactory situation were made in the early days of the war, when the Musicians' Union instituted new terms and the gramophone companies, acting tacitly but no less effectively in unison, refused them. The London players for whom these terms were sought were 'locked out' for nearly two years, and the companies carried on with orchestras from the provinces and reprints from America. This was uneconomic in many cases, but it had evidently been decided that the London players had to be beaten. Eventually, it became clear that the dispute was leading nowhere, and a compromise agreeable to the musicians was accepted.

At this point, at least one orchestra decided to make a further stand, not directly on behalf of individual players, but in the interest of the orchestral society itself. It was argued that if a certain recording sold well, especially in the United States at which most British recordings are directed, this must be due in some measure to the performance and reputation of the orchestra concerned. Therefore, a share of the profits, a royalty, should be paid to the orchestral society, just as it is paid to an author. This new proposal was met with a series of replies, all fully documented with relevant figures, aiming to show that this could only be done at the cost of bankrupting the gramophone company. When the arguments and figures had been digested, and the orchestra persisted in its claim, agreement was eventually reached, and justice began to be done. It is precisely this kind of long term arrangement which helps to make it possible for an orchestra to survive the many uncertainties of its career, and gramophone companies benefit by the close association with a well organized orchestra. But in a competitive commercial world such gains are secured with great difficulty and are threatened at every economic crisis.

New developments in the gramophone industry pose wide questions for the future. The advent of long playing records, for many years whispered to have been kept secretly behind locked doors, has brought a new element to the turntable which may prove revolutionary. Already it has adversely affected the market for the old type of disc, for it avoids the bugbear of changing the record at four-minute intervals (never satisfactorily accomplished by automatic methods) and, therefore, becomes a more serious competitor to the ease of the radio. Among keen-eared listeners, the bias had been for some time towards the gramophone, with its greater fidelity to instrumental tone and wider range of harmonic reproduction. Now, with the possibility of playing a whole symphony on one or two sides, the scales are tipped even further in that direction. But the end is not yet. Television may bring a plague on both their houses; and what further magic developments lie in wait for us all?

14 Concerts for Children

MUSIC as a subject in collective education is only a recent addition to the curriculum, and was an exception rather than the rule until well after the first world war. Indeed, music as a part of any boy's education was frowned upon by many authorities, and I can well remember the slighting and sarcastic remarks of a schoolmaster when I insisted on practising the violin for so many hours a day at the expense of the more brilliant, academic career which he had envisaged for me, and which would undoubtedly have brought more kudos to him and credit to the school. Had I written bad verse regularly instead of on widely-separated occasions, or produced drawings or paintings of questionable quality, he would certainly have approved of this, as something which came within his vision of culture; but scribbling music or playing the violin, although it might fill an awkward gap in the concert on Founder's Day, was no serious occupation for a healthy boy.

Perhaps I was particularly unfortunate, but it is true that the acceptance of music on the same level as other arts has a history of little more than thirty years. Since then, the practice of music and the teaching of musical appreciation in schools, supplemented by special broadcast programmes, have been given a certain status, and this was followed by public orchestral concerts with programmes specially designed to attract and interest the future generation of music lovers.

By 1939, considerable headway had been made, and an organization under the direction of Sir Robert Mayer was giving concerts in various centres with the best orchestra available, conducted by Sir Malcolm Sargent and certain young conductors. These concerts were always well attended, and school authorities vied with each other in sending representative groups. The easy and fluent explanations of the music and of the orchestral instruments which Sir Malcolm gave created a comfortable atmosphere and placed the young listeners on easy terms with what had often proved to be a fearsome subject of study.

As distinct from many schools of musical appreciation, the organizers of these concerts insisted that children should begin by enjoying music; listening to it without inhibitions and self-conscious thought. In this they differed vitally from the music appreciationists to whom a comprehension of the structure and bare bones of music sometimes seemed to be considered as a *sine qua non* of musical enjoyment. Some groups of children were indeed warned that on returning to their schools they would be expected to compose an account or criticism of the music they had heard. One can easily imagine the almost terrified concentration of the unfortunate children, attempting to grapple with an abstract succession of sounds, trying desperately to secure a hold and grasping nothing but the most extraneous and superficial details, unconsciously but effectively being prevented from enjoying the experience by the ill-advised enthusiasm of the didactic mind. It says much for Sir Malcolm that he threatened to veto the attendance of children from any school where this barbarian practice was in force, and it needed strong powers of persuasion to convince those concerned that they were blocking the entrance to the fairyland of music to the children committed to their charge. It may be that the purely formal appreciation of Shakespeare among many adults in this country can be traced to a similar failure to grasp the essential truth that the first step to any appreciation of art is simple enjoyment.

At the beginning of the war, many circumstances combined to render children's concerts impracticable. The chief of these was, of course, the large-scale evacuation of children with a corresponding break-up of the groups previously organized. The perilous position in which orchestras found themselves added to other difficulties, and the unwillingness of municipal and educational authorities to permit large gatherings of children almost convinced us that children's concerts were a thing of the past or, at best, of the future.

Eventually, however, schools settled down in their new homes, the risk of air-raids during school hours could be reasonably calculated, and the great decentralization of orchestral music began. It was not surprising to find that the valuable seed sown in the years before the war had thrown out roots which a careful cultivation could bring to maturity. The time for the full flowering is not yet, but there is enough evidence to show that with wise co-operation between educational authorities and symphonic organizations the future public can be prepared for an enlightened approach to what, for a great proportion of the present generation, has been a closed book.

The London Philharmonic Orchestra has, since 1940, given special concerts in a large number of provincial centres to audiences of children numbering, under favourable conditions, as many as three thousand in one hall. It began by admitting children to day-time concerts at special rates, but the demand for accommodation rapidly became so great that concerts devoted to children, with programmes and verbal analyses prepared for them, have become a regular feature of the Orchestra's work. If some of the children still find the concert boring they rarely show it, and if we admit, as I am loath to do, that only a reasonably small percentage display a lively interest, the work is still justified and would even then have an incalculable effect on the future of music in this country. And who can tell what value such an experience may have when it is matured in the magic store-room of a child's memory?

There is little doubt, then, as to the value of such opportunities for the children, but since this book is devoted chiefly to the problem of maintaining symphony orchestras in England in the present and the future, we should explore the possibilities of co-operation between symphony organizations and educational authorities. The possible scope of children's concerts is no narrower than that of concerts in general, for no scheme will become effective unless the opportunities offered to the children of listening to music are made regular, if not too frequent. To the lay mind, there would seem to be no reason why so many hours each term should not be allotted for listening to symphonic music. In some schools the wireless is now used for a similar purpose, and a combination of the two, with a wise employment of gramophone records, would be invaluable. In any national financial plan for the maintenance of symphony orchestras, educational authorities might well take a part which, though modest enough in relation to its worth to their children, would provide no little help to the musicians concerned, provided that all concerts were arranged in effective conjunction with full concerts in the respective centres.

Much has been done along these lines since the end of the war. In almost every centre where an orchestra has been established, children's concerts have become an integral part of its work and of its financial plan. Local educational authorities have, in the main, grasped the opportunities offered by the existence of an orchestra, and municipalities have also become aware of this new trend. The London County Council has, for example, been responsible for offering twenty concerts each year to its own children, and will continue this work in spite of drastic and ill-judged economies in its other musical activities.

Wide schemes of this kind would offer considerable new scope for young conductors. The children would naturally be encouraged to attend these concerts primarily to listen to the orchestra and not, as is so often the case with their elders, to watch the conductor, and a young man or woman whose sympathies were in the work could adequately present the music to the children and acquire valuable experience of orchestra and audience in so doing. Obviously, not every young and gifted conductor would have the consummate ease and fluency of Sir Malcolm Sargent in speaking to the children, and it might be necessary to prepare and train a panel of speakers to take over this part of the proceedings, but this division of labour would create no great difficulty; it might, on the contrary, produce a number of capable lecturers who could be sent round the country in advance of an orchestra, giving talks on forth-coming programmes. Similar introductions to programmes have already taken place in certain favoured towns, and if the scheme grows to cover the whole country many more lecturers will be needed.

Children's concerts have become, then, a recognized part of school curricula, and although their future may tremble as educational grants are reduced they are likely to survive. It must be remembered, however, that their direct effect ceases as the child leaves school, and from the age of fifteen he is left unguided to his own devices. Plagued with American musical nonsense wherever he goes, his real musical memory may soon become dull and tarnished, the energy of the orchestra smoothed over to the tired monotony of 'swing'. What can be done to preserve the musical curiosity we once aroused?

For many years, a few of us have tried to persuade English musical, educational, municipal, and academic circles to interest themselves in a fascinating experiment carried on since 1940 in Belgium, France, and a number of other countries. The 'Jeunesses Musicales' is a grouping of adolescents who, with adult guidance largely replaced by juvenile talent and enthusiasm, enjoy special performances each year. For nominal payments they have admission to symphony concerts, chamber music performances, and lectures, they publish their own magazines and arrange their own displays, compete in choirs and orchestras, and generally get all the knowledge and all the fun of music by the most natural methods. Already the membership in these countries reaches many thousands, and anyone with direct experience of these movements will not easily forget either the enthusiasm of these youngsters, or the seriousness of their intentions. They have bridged the gap between schooldays and maturity, and the effect on the musical future of their countries is certain, if incalculable.

In our country, little has been done. Independently, similar movements are getting under way in one or two cities, notably in Liverpool, where conditions are favourable and an active disciple is busy. Elsewhere, excuses take the place of initiative, and the clear advantage of carrying on what has been done in school years is being lost. Yet this movement can do more than anything else in forming the lasting mass audience we are aiming to build. The challenge is there for those who care to accept it.

15 *The Finance of a Modern Orchestra*

IT will have been seen already that from the time of the foundation of what may be called the modern orchestra some form of subsidy has always been necessary. The subvention may have come from one of a variety of sources; from a king or prince who had a taste for music or a desire for display, as in the case of Louis XIV and Lully; from a municipality or central government, as in the case of Sibelius; from the coffers of a wealthy man with ambitions as a conductor, and who wanted an orchestra of his own, as I have mentioned in an earlier chapter; from a group of business men who, for more obscure reasons, think this a good way of spending money, as is done in the U.S.A., or, last of all, from an organization like the B.B.C. which, in spite of its occasional arrogance and 'old school tie' manner, is in its turn maintained by the humble pound notes of its millions of listeners.

In England, the B.B.C. and rare municipalities apart, we had always pinned our faith to private enterprise; groups of socially minded and generous people have banded themselves together, like the founders of the Royal Philharmonic Society, have pooled their resources, and by means of their organization have been able to promote symphony concerts and provide splendid opportunities for composers. Such organizations have seldom operated on lines broad enough to make a permanent orchestra possible, although, with the help of interested business people, an air of permanence had been given to certain orchestras from time to time. One of the most recent examples was, as I have related earlier, the pre-war London Philharmonic Orchestra, which took over the glory and responsibility of the preceding Royal Philharmonic Orchestra which had functioned for this sole purpose during the previous century.

To maintain a permanent symphony orchestra, to put eighty players on a salary basis with the normal privileges of professional workers, will cost to-day, at a modest estimate, upwards of £70,000 per annum. A slightly smaller orchestra might do valuable work, while one which was expected to do justice to the demands of the greatest modern music would need at least thirty players more than the number I have stipulated; but for practical purposes an orchestra of eighty musicians would satisfy our needs. The problem of how to find such a sum of money, which makes no allowance for conductors' fees, rents, travel, printing, publicity, and so on, is no less pressing to-day than ever it was.

At present, and probably for some time to come, symphony orchestras have to follow a semi-commercial career. The major part of their income must be derived from the proceeds of engagements or from concerts promoted by their own organizations. This income will always remain an uncertain quantity unless, under a musical dictator, audiences are dragooned and regimented into filling a hall whenever a concert is given. Which God forbid! So many conditions militate against definite financial results from concert-giving that no prophecy of profits can ever be made. On rare occasions, when the appearance of a well-known symphony orchestra and a famous conductor is turned into a social event, such high prices of admission can be charged that concert agents find these affairs extremely profitable, but even then their fat cigars, champagne, and saloon cars come chiefly from the skilled handling of a few tenors and solo instrumentalists who make brief but golden descents upon this country. In recent times, however, the general level of admission prices is being driven down by the force of circumstances until, with a corresponding rise in overhead expenses, a series of concerts is almost certain to end in a deficit.

The total cost of running an orchestra is well in excess of twice what it was only ten years ago, and when receipts are accepted as being lower than they were then it will not be difficult to guess at the resulting gap between income and expenditure. This is the permanent problem of the symphony orchestra, and until it is solved we shall never know from one year to the next whether this or that orchestra will succeed in overcoming this obstacle to security and forward planning. An orchestra meeting only from time to time when it is engaged for a concert by an outside body which accepts the financial responsibility will avoid the danger of financial disaster; on the other hand, it will not fulfil the functions which are essential to a real orchestra. This matter is dealt with in my final chapter.

To take an orchestra of eighty men round the country, or abroad on an ambassadorial tour, going from town to town each day, is to be held up to ransom at every turn. It is all in keeping with recognized commercial standards, but full of threats to artistic ones. Railway fares, even after such slight concessions as are sometimes made, become a serious burden; a sixth of the receipts for the week may be swallowed up in this way. Journeys by road represent a considerable economy, but impose an added strain on the players which often affects the evening performance. When each night has to be spent in a different town, accommodation in the first hotel with room to spare has to be taken, at a tariff which, steeply increased since the war and multiplied by the number of players, assumes terrifying proportions, perhaps another sixth of the receipts. From the remaining two-thirds must come the costs of advertising the concerts; handbills, posters, newspaper columns, and various incidental expenses, which, however generous, always leave some members of the public in the position of pleading that had they known a concert was to take place they would have been there. The rent of the hall, commission for agents, attendants, and other local people whose help has been called in – all, all must be paid before the turn of the musician comes, and I have not mentioned the hire of music, the charge for permission to perform copyright works, or the comparatively princely fees of the conductor.

It happens not infrequently, especially when the hall is small, that when all these claims have been met there is little or nothing left for those who have actually organized and given the concert. *Giving* a concert is an inspired phrase! Obviously, a wise committee of management will only undertake a series of concerts which show, at least on paper, satisfactory prospects, but no branch of social science has yet devised a formula for gauging the size or value of an audience in advance. There are people who have a flair for foretelling the reaction of a certain town to this or that entertainment, but one cannot rely too safely on such intuition – or bankrupt impresarios could not exist! And if an orchestra takes its social duties seriously it will be bound to include in its itineraries some towns of modest halls and limited populations which have a right, if only for this reason, to hear the best music. But visits of this kind will offer only the barest working margin, a margin which may disappear at the first breath of the unexpected.

The ordinary member of an audience, seeing every seat filled in his local hall, will be quite confident that the orchestra has done very well out of it and may wonder what happens to all the profits. He is not to be blamed for this error. A thousand people seen at a glance represent potential wealth to the untrained eye. In box-office receipts their total contributions are woefully small. Let us assume that the average price of admission is four shillings, and this is high in a suburban district where the best seat at the cinema costs less. The total capacity figure cannot exceed £200, from which must be deducted the rent of the hall, printing, advertising, poster display, cost of stewards, and the agent's commission. If this is estimated at £60, we are being modest. An average fee for a conductor may be put at £40, although this may be reduced if the risk of an unknown name is taken. The £100 remaining has to cover the cost of the orchestra, and seventy musicians at the minimum rate established by the Musicians' Union will have to be paid £160. Overhead administrative expenses, and the general running cost of a permanent organization have not yet been mentioned. And it has been assumed that the hall is near enough to the orchestra's centre to avoid the added expense of travelling and hotels.

It will be seen from this that the symphony orchestra offers no inducement to the cautious investor; in the long run, considerable sums of money must be lost, just as they are 'lost' on education, art galleries, museums, public parks, and a number of other apparently unproductive amenities.

The cautious investor would, of course, advise against giving concerts in such small halls. On any commercial assessment, who could gainsay him? But what a cultural heresy! Can we believe that because a citizen lives in a community possessing only a hall of these dimensions he is not entitled to a privilege enjoyed by those who live by chance in a great city? Does the ability to appreciate music depend on a mathematical equation of population? If it did, our leading orchestras could stay profitably in their own cities, and the Royal Albert Hall, with the addition of the Royal Festival Hall, could amply support as many orchestras as London could provide. In truth, genuine and knowledge-able appreciation is often more easily found in small communities, where local patriotism and civic sense are more highly developed than in great cities. I state this with regret, as a Londoner bred and born. In the last few months, I have seen a splendid Nottingham audience welcome the *Requiem* of Fauré, a foregone failure in Kensington, and the Central Hall, Chatham, crowded to the utmost limits for a performance of Vaughan Williams' *London Symphony* which, two days earlier, had attracted in hard cash one third of that spent for the same purpose in Chatham. It is difficult to regard financial profit or loss as the relevant factor in such comparisons.

From this it is an obvious step for all those who consider the best music to be an essential part of our social life to say that the State should find the money, and during the last ten years some valuable advances have been made in this direction. But although the amount concerned is trivial in comparison with the astronomical sums commonly discussed in Government circles, and although there are already signs that our rulers are becoming conscious of the claims of music, steps so far taken have been tentative and may go into retreat as economic conditions worsen. It cannot be said that the cultural importance of the symphony orchestra has ever been realized by them. Perhaps it is that in this 'nation of shopkeepers' we only appreciate something tangible. We will make a special grant to secure a certain painting for a national gallery, or spend money on preserving an historic building or to outbid the American market in an endeavour to retain an invaluable book or document for one of our museums, and indeed no one will quarrel with such awareness of real values. But music is so vague a thing. Sound in motion. And as soon as the concert is over, what is there to show for it? Absolutely nothing, for the emotional, intellectual, and spiritual satisfaction derived from the experience may bear no fruit for many years, and when it does, who can trace the stimulus so far back to its source?

There have been even deeper reasons for this official neglect of music. Governing circles in Great Britain have not, since the rise of the symphony orchestra, displayed any great interest in, or sympathy for, music; even to Queen Victoria and Prince Albert we are indebted only for an exaggerated valuation of Mendelssohn. We have been blessed with no princelings who, with their eyes turned towards Versailles, have used their orchestras as a medium for an ostentatious display of wealth, power, and culture. Although the motive for such expenditure may have been fundamentally vulgar, composers whose glory far outshines that of their patrons produced magnificent works as a result, displaying their own splendour rather than the temporal brilliance of those whom they served.

Deprived of such exalted assistance, British musical organization, typified at its highest by the symphony orchestra, has languished. Perhaps one could scarcely expect cultural sympathy from coal owners, steel kings, and the higher middlemen of commerce, and it is only now, when the upward rush of industrialism has eased, that their descendants, standing aloof from their family origins, have the leisure to interest themselves in more polite activities. Thus it is that we find occasional benefactors to whom a thousand pounds gift to an orchestra is not considered ill-spent money, or others who will establish or subsidize an orchestra which will satisfy their desires and, sometimes, their talents as conductors. To such people, whose number is rapidly being diminished by taxation, orchestras have been grateful, and even to-day the practical value of such help cannot be denied. But it offers no sure foundation for a permanent orchestra. The wealthy donor may change the object of his favour at any moment, like the noble marquis who, after having partly erected a handsome Anglican church at his own expense, suddenly turned Catholic and left the unfinished ghost of his former sympathies to mock his infidelity. Conductors have been known to desert one orchestra for another when the response to their largesse has been inadequate, and there must always be the tendency for such a conductor to gain a power of economic life and death over his players, and this, unsound and unhealthy in the eighteenth century, is an anachronism to-day.

While millionaires exist, they may do far worse than subsidize orchestras, as is done so often in the United States, and municipalities may be shamed into their responsibilities by such actions. In the same way, one of the finest achievements of the B.B.C. has been its symphony orchestra, which set a standard of permanence and of artistic daring which no private organization could have done earlier. It also demonstrated what could be done when steady financial support made it possible to place musicians on full-time contracts, engage a full-time conductor to train them, and prepare programmes upon which a definite style and standard of playing could be built.

In spite of this example, it was some time before official action was taken in the direction indicated by this experiment, and this action lagged behind public feeling. When, in February and July, 1940, the London Philharmonic found itself on its financial beam-ends, it decided to make the fact public and to appeal to music-lovers for help. The first appeal, launched by the eloquence of Sir Thomas Beecham, revealed a condition of things which was not generally known or understood, and the response was encouraging, not only for the reason that the Orchestra was saved for six months, but because the social conscience of at least a section of the public was aroused. Later, Mr J. B. Priestley appealed to his own many followers with an even greater result, and the combination of these two efforts proved that there were thousands of people in England to whom the existence of a first-class symphony orchestra was a matter of tremendous moment, even when they themselves were rarely able to enjoy the pleasure of listening to it. Assuming, as one safely can, that quite as many more people, whom only inertia prevented from responding to the appeals, shared these feelings, we have a body of opinion which can be considered as representative. It is probably true that, at the period when the appeals were made, the development of the 'total' war was making many cultured members of the nation apprehensive for the values which they held most dear, and that their response to the appeal to save the L.P.O. crystallized those feelings. On the part which a government would play in connexion with the work of cultural bodies which have justified their existence and their methods of organization, I shall have more to say in the following chapter.

A symphony orchestra presents problems which can be approached sympathetically and with understanding only by those who belong, and who have, over a period of years, identified themselves with the desires, the frustrations, and the grumbles of the musicians who compose it. For this reason, no external body of men, however gifted in the details of concert organization and what is known as orchestral management, will win the trust and confidence of the players and all that these words imply. When you have worked with musicians you realize not only their pettiness and absurdities, but the fine qualities which are rarely revealed, and never to external bureaucrats.

There is no doubt that a symphony orchestra whose elected committee is given a free hand with its affairs and its finances will make mistakes which will cause a business man to hold up his hands in pious horror; the first six months of the L.P.O. – for which I was partly responsible – was a succession of them, but who cares? They were not cold-blooded, *ignorant* mistakes, but came from over-excitement, too much enthusiasm, and a confidence born from the knowledge that the Orchestra was sailing boldly down the stream of the twentieth century and not drifting in the back-water of a bygone epoch.

And what is six months of error to a permanent orchestra, laying the foundations for an organization which has to persist through wars, famine, revolution, and history?

16 *Conclusions*

'The only true prophets are those who carve out the future which they announce.' – JAMES CONNOLLY

OF those readers who have suffered with not too much impatience the expression of my dissatisfactions and criticisms of our musical institutions some may have wondered at the drift of the arguments, whether indeed I have been hitting out wildly in all directions, or whether the blows were ultimately aimed at a single target. At the risk of boring the more discerning, who will have seen through all my strictures against conductors, patrons, Government departments, and so on, I must endeavour to correlate my opinions on these and similar matters, if only to satisfy myself that I have not scribbled off a few unrelated chapters to ease the grudges of many years. There is so much in our life to-day which we feel to be fruitless and exasperating, so little which, for all our prattle of 'new worlds', is positively constructive, that it is easy for our disapproval to become merely a sign of our impotence, a specious satisfaction gained by the mere venting of a superficial displeasure.

Such satisfaction, like patriotism and other 'refuges of a scoundrel', is not enough. That we should go on being displeased with things as they are, long after the rebellious twenties, is an excellent attitude and was never more necessary than to-day, but such feelings must be the prelude to some hard thinking which, in its turn, will be of very little use unless it leads to a plan of action combined with a determination to put the plan into operation.

Few people will disagree with this as far as it goes, but most of us are so occupied with quotidian details, living as it were from hand to mouth, that we may almost be excused if we lose sight of the very aim we originally made for. But now the world changes before our very eyes; institutions, prejudices, and hampering traditions are crumbling around us, and even while we attempt to resist or to control these changes, hoping in either event to save ourselves from becoming engulfed in the ruins, we have unexampled opportunities of planning and erecting the structures which are to take their place. And from the falling edifices we can select certain bricks and stones which may usefully be employed in our new buildings, and the best of the past will serve another and even better purpose. We must build with the same confidence in the permanence of our future which went to the erection of churches, cathedrals, and those old stone barns and farmhouses of Devon which were meant to outlive their builders.

The orchestras of Great Britain have, as we have seen, already started along new lines; not the same lines in each case, but those which run out from the past without diverting the future. The loss of pre-war patrons, pre-war organization, and some pre-war engagements may be considered as one link in a chain of changing conditions which, already frequent, must be taken as a rule for the future. At the same time, the search for new audiences, the consequent and urgent need for more and better concert halls, an internal constitution and a method of stabilization are the prerequisites of the new conditions. We have now in our country the makings of several bodies which can be dignified by the title of 'modern orchestras'. In their different methods of organization there are many points of dissimilarity, and if I were to claim that of the London Philharmonic as being superior to the others (as I should do if I were challenged), those in charge of other orchestras could doubtless produce arguments in proof of the contrary. Time will settle the validity of either claim, but long before it has been settled, all will have achieved a magnificent work for the art of music.

In doing this work, these modern organizations must be prepared for further change, or their modernity will be but short-lived. At every step by which they adapt themselves to meet existing conditions, such adaptations must be made with an eye on future developments. Like a billiard player who, in making a successful stroke, does not fail to bear in mind the manner in which the balls are to be left; in making each stroke he will prepare for the next. Some such ideas have been at the basis of the direction of the L.P.O. since September 1939, and other orchestras which have become permanent in the meantime deal with their affairs in similar ways. But the successes of the new ideas have exposed a weakness and a danger. Once started upon its new lines, the L.P.O. became, like the Vienna Philharmonic, a *Kunstrepublik*, an artistic republic which maintained its integrity in spite of the praise of its admirers and the sneers of its denigrators. Another orchestra may have a 'monarchy' in the form of a celebrated conductor or a leading citizen as chairman, but to live by either method as a 'closed state' and to attempt to ignore external conditions soon discloses a fundamental weakness in the musical organization of Great Britain which must be corrected if the future is to be given enduring qualities. Isolation must lead to competition and antagonism, and the keynote of musical advance is co-operation on nothing less than a national basis.

Here someone will whisper, 'Ah, yes, a Ministry of Fine Arts,' and twenty-five years or so ago such a whispered suggestion might have received ready support, but the dangers of external control in this and other spheres have become only too apparent, while the virtues and strength of self-organized bodies lead us to believe that here lies the future type of organization.

In the first place, the practice of music for the last ten years has revealed a surprising capacity for leadership among musicians themselves, a capacity which in earlier days was seldom demanded and therefore seldom came to light. The resuscitation of musical activities and the introduction of many novel ideas soon after the outbreak of the last war, for example, were solely due to practising musicians; had this initiative not been displayed it is doubtful whether any music would have survived the war in an organized fashion, and the highly developed mechanism of the symphony orchestra would have been one of the first casualties.

The war-time recovery of the L.P.O., the stimulating activities of Dame Myra Hess at the National Gallery, and the impressive resilience of the London Symphony Orchestra, showed what could be done. Other organizations displayed the same qualities to a greater or lesser degree and, given reasonable facilities, it is not too much to suppose that the whole musical planning of the country may safely be left to the musicians themselves, to those who know from their own personal and practical experience what are the problems and how they can best be solved. That they can be helped by the experience and specialized knowledge of those who act as concert agents, promoters, and impresarios, is true enough, but it has been painfully evident that in difficult situations the initiative passes almost completely from their hands into those of musicians to whom the furtherance of musical life is essential for existence. In short, to those to whom music matters more than anything else in the world.

Such facilities as are needed to enable a national plan for music to be made come naturally from some form of

Government grant or subsidy, especially when one is dealing with the symphony orchestra, and during the last few years welcome signs have shown that this is the direction our musical life is taking. Before considering what steps have been taken, and in what ways the fullest benefits may be made to accrue from them, it must be said that a Ministry of Fine Arts would prove to be one of the least satisfactory forms of administration and control. Its name alone betrays it. It connotes a Minister, a gentleman moved by political exigencies, liable to be changed and replaced at any time for reasons not always connected with his abilities, a possible victim of cliques and cabals, and a rallying point for the artistic intrigues and jealousies which have marred the history of subsidized music in France and Germany. Secondly, 'of Fine Arts'. I contend that this term, obsolete except in its application to the precious wares of the collector, has little significance for us. This in spite of the repeated dictum of one moving on the fringe of the musical profession that 'music must be considered as a fine art, and can never be enjoyed by more than a few'; in spite of the popular fallacy that at the announcement of a concert of serious music most people switch their wireless sets into silence. Music can, and will, be enjoyed by a growing mass of people in this country, providing only that we offer them the best within our power to give.

As far as symphony orchestras are concerned, grants and subsidies must be administered from a professional, if not an industrial, point of view. This is probably no less true of other branches of our musical life, but I cannot presume to understand their particular problems, for which they will find the appropriate answer. For the orchestra, as I have mentioned earlier, the responsibility for all administration must rest with the organization itself, of which its most experienced and trusted members, elected by their colleagues, will acquire skill and knowledge, and display imagination enough to guide their own organization along a successful course. This opinion, which I held even before the war, has been strengthened and justified by the L.P.O. experience of the last eleven years. The L.P.O. was able to overcome its main organizational problems before official help became available, but it has been seen that other methods of dealing with these problems have failed or are threatened with failure in spite of outside aid. The explanation of this must be sought.

Government help to music began in a tentative manner and as far as symphony orchestras are concerned, is still carried on without conviction. C.E.M.A. was formed in the early days of the war to satisfy a temporary need arising from the dislocation of normal musical life. When it was re-formed into the Arts Council of Great Britain, it approach to our national problems was changed, and with increased funds (which are still relatively small) it gave more help to symphony orchestras. At the same time, the source of these funds was taken over from the Ministry of Education by the Treasury, and, while the worse faults of a Ministry of Fine Arts have been avoided, certain bureaucratic tendencies have become evident. Appointments to leading positions are always made of 'safe' people, of those who conform socially and politically to a given norm. This can only mean that the administration is often deprived of outstanding ability, for in the musical world special gifts are seldom found against a background of accepted social or political thinking.

Arts Council policy has shown itself passive rather than active. Correctly wishing to avoid direct interference with the organizations to which it grants money, it has proved incapable of positive planning, unwilling to use its power in guiding the wider lines of musical developments, and waiting on the initiative of others before taking action of any kind. It has been the central mistake to assume that these reticences are of the same nature. I have always insisted that the Arts Council should not interfere with the internal policy of an orchestra, and that its rights were properly exercised when an observer was sent to meetings of the management committees to see how affairs were being conducted, and to satisfy himself that public money was being reasonably spent. But to regard this disinclination to dictate internal policy as demanding an equal caution in dealing with policy between orchestras, or between them and their public, is the very negation of its obvious responsibilities.

Once official support has been granted to orchestras, putting them beyond the crippling fear of bankruptcy and dissolution, when it has enabled them to take a longer view of their external activities and internal organization, and when they can plan on a scale commensurate with the high standard of their artistic development, their work will still be seriously hampered if each orchestra regards itself as a separate body, fearful and therefore jealous of the success and progress of other orchestras.

That any orchestra will wish to remain autonomous, building up in its own way an individual style of performance and general character, is natural and not unhealthy, but that each should be divorced from and antagonistic to the other will be fatal to the task of taking music to the widest possible audience. Some form of national organization will be found essential.

Already, the permanent orchestras have done something for themselves by the formation of a National Association of Symphony Orchestras, representing the joint interests of the City of Birmingham Symphony Orchestra, the Hallé, the Liverpool Philharmonic, the Bournemouth Municipal, the London Philharmonic, the London Symphony, and the Scottish National Orchestra. Many questions of co-ordination have been satisfactorily dealt with, and common problems with other bodies successfully overcome. They have also linked themselves with other musical authorities in an Orchestral Employers' Association which, if it began with something of an anti-Musicians' Union bias, has not allowed it to develop or to prevent it from carrying out valuable reforms. In the metropolis, the London Concerts Co-ordination Association has come into being with the expressed intention of bringing order into the chaos of music-making in the capital's principal halls.

This proliferation of committees represents a nightmare to busy orchestral administrators, but the difficulties which called them into being were even more terrifying. And since the sovereignty of each member-organization is carefully respected, the opportunities of discussing mutual problems are invaluable. Under existing conditions, these bodies have a heterogeneous complexion, for they contain elected members of democratic orchestras, arbitrarily selected officials of the more old-fashioned type of organization, and even certain municipal officers. This is not a bad thing, for no one method of organization will provide all the right answers, and each may learn a great deal from the other.

In spite of all that has been done in these ways, the main tasks of seeing Britain's music as a whole still remains to be tackled. Here, one would have thought, was the place for the Arts Council. But, apart from giving its general blessing, and granting occasional facilities for meetings, the Council holds itself aloof, observing it all with a distant if paternal eye. This is a matter for regret. Behind this over-modest attitude there is, no doubt, a genuine fear of over-centralization, and this fear would be generally shared by those who see the only healthy future for our music in spreading activities and responsibilities all over the country. But only such a body as the Arts Council, financially responsible to most of the members of the committees I have mentioned, has the prestige and the disinterestedness needed to weave all the strands passing through its hands into a shapely pattern.

If the Arts Council itself continues to decline the onus of such responsibility, it might even better take the lead in forming yet another body, representative of all those concerned, and giving it such power as was needed to study the national position and to relate the various regional elements in a practical scheme. For this, advice on the broadest basis would be required, and it is here that the Arts Council often fails. It has panels on the several arts under its guidance, but weakens itself by an arbitrary refusal to invite on to a panel anyone belonging to an organization which benefits from an Arts Council grant. It must be clear that, since all reputable symphonic organizations receive such grants, expert opinion on orchestral administration is carefully excluded. So that on relevant matters Arts Council deliberations start from scratch.

The first question to be faced by a central orchestral council would be how best to cover the whole of the country, and bring music within reasonable reach of everyone. In this, it would have to stamp out the heresy which claims that a wireless performance is an adequate substitute for a real concert, and all that can be expected by anyone living at any distance from the great centres of population. The value of broadcast music is very great, and the present increased demand for symphony concerts owes a debt to the B.B.C., but in developing interest and enthusiasm for orchestral performances, the wireless is only useful to those to whom actual concerts are a living memory of which a broadcast concert renews details and stimulates recollection. Only when orchestral concerts are widely given will the wireless come into its own.

With notable exceptions, this is now coming true. Since the later days of the war, permanent orchestras have been created in many regions: Yorkshire, Lancashire (Manchester and Liverpool), Birmingham, Bournemouth, are all served in their main centres and outlying towns, while Scotland, formerly with a seasonal orchestra only, has recently formed the Scottish National Orchestra and, in doing so, promises to settle the feud between Glasgow and Edinburgh. Nevertheless, wide areas are still neglected.

We are apt to forget, for instance, that it is rare for the inhabitants of Wales to hear an orchestral concert without coming to England for the purpose. It is true that in 1928 a National Orchestra of Wales was formed, and for three years and a half did admirable work in Cardiff, Swansea, Llanelly, and many other centres in South Wales. It was, I believe, the first orchestra in Great Britain to perform all the symphonies of Sibelius, and programmes covering all the important orchestral works were offered to a growing, enthusiastic public. In addition, a group of members of the Orchestra, assured of an income by their engagement, were able to organize a regular series of chamber-music concerts in Cardiff and elsewhere, and in the course of a few years succeeded in building up an appreciative and discriminating audience for this branch of music. But the problems of orchestral organization and finance were too much for the bodies supporting the N.O.W., and this gallant attempt was allowed to become no more than a thrilling memory to those who had attended its concerts regularly, and to whom music had been given a personal meaning. As a member of this ill-fated band I can answer for the tremendous effect it had on the musical taste of its many young listeners, who were led to seek every opportunity of hearing an orchestra, and who have always spoken of the N.O.W. with the deepest regret.

The Music Development Committee of the Musicians' Union has now put forward a plan which, if accepted locally, will take up once again the challenge in Wales. In this, the Committee has made a well-timed approach. When the National Orchestra of Wales was fighting its losing battle only the help of the various municipalities could have saved it. But they had no legal powers to spend the ratepayers' money on a cultural matter. It was not, indeed, until 1948 that an Act of Parliament was passed containing a clause which enabled them to do so. To-day (February 1951) fifty local authorities of South Wales have met and agreed that an orchestra for South Wales is desirable. Furthermore, they are not shocked at the suggestion that the orchestra will have to be guaranteed from the rates. This is an advance, indeed.

The powers permitted by this notable Act of Parliament will, if widely used, effect a revolution in the musical life of Great Britain. Already, most of our cities, and many smaller towns, have accepted some cultural responsibility. Permanent orchestras like the Hallé, the Liverpool Philharmonic, and the City of Birmingham Symphony Orchestra, for example, receive annual grants from the authority of their principal city, and in addition are given financial assistance in a lesser degree by an increasing proportion of those towns in their region where concerts are given.

Here we have the future basis for our work, a tripartite basis, indicative of how that work is carried out. If orchestras were supported solely from a kind of Ministry of Fine Arts they would run all the dangers I have mentioned earlier, for, however fine the original intentions, political demands must eventually intrude into this purely cultural question. With the responsibility of finding the money divided between three different types of authority, satisfying different claims and intentions, a much closer relation with reality is maintained. Arts Council grants and, to a lesser extent, those from the City fathers, are given with the main intention of enabling the particular orchestra to maintain the necessary number of players, allow for adequate rehearsal, provide a reasonably attractive contract to the players, and to go towards meeting the inevitable discrepancy between box-office receipts and current expenses. Grants from smaller towns, however, are almost all in direct recognition of services rendered. Municipal councils, especially when they possess a suitable town hall, are sensitive to the demand for good concerts made by their citizens and young people, and are glad of the new Act which allows them to satisfy it. There are still some, of course, to whom expenditure of this kind is an unjustified extravagance; to whom the town hall must be a source of revenue to reduce the rates, and projects which limit this reduction are to be frowned upon. Such diehards, who, incidentally, are to be found in various political groupings, will disappear as time goes on and as the cultural movement becomes general.

Local authorities who have had no experience of dealings with the musical world are sometimes at a loss to know how to begin. The Arts Council has a certain amount of information within its reach, which it will dispense when asked to do so, but it is an organization of musicians, the Music Development Committee, which has, so far, taken the initiative in stimulating local councils in this direction. It has already achieved encouraging results, but by its nature it is not the body to co-ordinate all that is being built up day after day throughout the country. There is still a serious need for such a body, one which can assess the musical needs of the country and the material existing for satisfying them.

As it is, the different regions live in almost complete musical isolation, apart from occasional interchanges of orchestras, and from the administrative meetings mentioned earlier. If relations between them were closer, and if they agreed to enter into some wider plan, I believe that an enormous amount of money would be saved. I am not advocating a pooling of resources, or any loss of independence, but a combined approach to a number of common problems. We must not sit back, feeling that the future of music is now guaranteed with public money, when still so much remains to be done, when still our audiences are relatively so small. The success of one orchestra or another must not blind us to the fact that symphonic music is in a precarious situation. That there are many encouraging features I have indicated already; but when every orchestra is dangerously near the edge of insolvency in spite of the funds placed at its disposal; when audiences are spasmodic and liable to be attracted more by famous names than by a genuine curiosity, and when too many municipal authorities look upon orchestral music with the blank stare of indifference or intolerance, complacency is unforgivable. I do not believe these perplexities can be met effectively by each orchestra separately, for the problems are national, and every branch of our cultural life can make a contribution to the ultimate solution if an effective lead is given.

*

While we are concentrating on these matters from the purely orchestral point of view, we must not fail to realize the scope which would be provided in other directions. At the present time, the number of our effective orchestral conductors is a small one. It is true that, with the establishment of more permanent orchestras the number has increased, but opportunities are severely limited. And if an orchestra wishes to raise its standard of playing in a short time, recourse has to be made to a foreigner. While we have been grateful to the help which has come to us from abroad, we have allowed our dependence to go on too long.

It is not enough to sit back and say that the British temperament is unsuitable for this occupation. One may talk of a national temperament after studying the reactions of the country as a whole, but within any nation most variations of temperament are to be found. Look, for example, at our own conductors: Beecham and Wood, Barbirolli and Boult, Heward and Harty, all splendid exponents of the art, and all so dissimilar. No, we must look for causes elsewhere. They lie in training and opportunity.

I believe that few of our young men are brought up with the right approach to the job. The world's greatest conductors accept their career as a lifetime of study. To them the concert is no more than the proof of their ability, which is more tellingly displayed at rehearsals and in their own private study of scores, acoustics, halls, instruments – and people. Half an hour with Koussevitzky, when a veteran of seventy-five with all the energy, enthusiasm, and curiosity of a youth, revealed this fact. He is no exception among the great. At eighty-four, Toscanini presents a new symphony of Vaughan Williams, learnt from memory, when he might with no apology rest upon the laurels of a lifetime. I rarely encounter such qualities in our own young men. It is not that they are lazy, incompetent, or unmusical, but they have not been made aware of the obligations of their profession. They are not exacting in their demands. If a concert promoter apologizes for the necessity of restricting preparation to one rehearsal, they wrinkle their brows and accept the inevitable. Anyone trained in the continental school would refuse calmly or violently, according to mood, and leave the performance to someone more accommodating. And he would be justified. But then, few of our young men have learnt how to rehearse and are even embarrassed by having too much time at their disposal. Nevertheless, there is no lack of talent among our musicians.

I have tried earlier in this book to sketch the plight of the young conductor who, in search of the experience without which he cannot secure engagements, is often driven to America – or despair. One of the aims of our orchestral council would be to restore a healthy balance between conductor and orchestra in the eyes of concert-goers so that they would not need to be tempted by a conductor with a well-advertised personality before coming to hear a concert. During the war, when we were thrown back upon our own resources, those conductors who remained in the country, reliable musicians if unspectacular, attracted the largest and most consistent audiences ever seen in Great Britain. And programmes began to move off the beaten track. It meant, simply, that the public was turning its attention to the orchestra, and to the music. Since 1945, the trend has been in the other direction again; the star conductor has dazzled us all, and the manner of music-making threatens to hide the matter.

This is no plea for isolationism. It is simply that we must take stock of the whole situation, and base our sense of values on the music itself, putting brilliance of orchestral playing and the hypnotic powers of certain conductors into their due place in the picture. We must remember, in and out of season, that music must not be expected to give us the thrills of a circus or the astonishment of a conjuring show. It must be part of our life, a food for our spirit, calling for the luxury of refinement only to heighten the enjoyment of more normal fare. Those concert-goers who restrict their visits to performances conducted by the most famous figures are not music lovers; they are either specialists in appreciation of orchestral playing, receptacles of propaganda, or plain snobs. And they will not even save the orchestral playing they claim to admire.

It is certain that opportunities for our own young men would increase substantially to-morrow if the public bought tickets on the valuation of the musical programme, and then settled down to enjoy it. How often concert planners play with the idea of giving young so-and-so a series of concerts; then shake their heads ruefully and say: 'No, we can't risk it. The hall will be half empty'. How gladly they would print his name over satisfying programmes if the public demanded music first and foremost.

I am not denying that a great conductor reveals more of the music; nor am I attempting to dismiss the highest orchestral standards as unimportant. But I have heard famous conductors greeted with cheers for slipshod work, and a less-known youngster ignored for a performance of intensity and clarity.

There is an economic side to this, too. It has been the common practice, and one generally accepted by the conductor, to allot a considerable fee to the man in front of the orchestra. This fee may vary from twenty to five hundred guineas for a concert, according to whether the conductor is a tyro or a Toscanini. No one else in the orchestra is paid half as much as the lower fee, and a conductor in the higher range is placed in a different class from his playing colleagues. The greatest evil is that it creates a small ring of conductors, leaving those outside little to hope for beyond an occasional emergency engagement which, while it may offer him a similar fee, denies him any continuity of experience, but provides every encouragement for disillusionment and its attendant ills.

These inflated fees are quite artificial. It has been known for a conductor to demand a fee 'higher than so-and-so received', and this spiral reaches astronomical levels. Prestige fees of this order bear no relation to the conductor's needs, and represent a crippling burden on the orchestral society, and a nest egg for the Inland Revenue. The value of a great conductor is admittedly beyond price to a fine orchestra, but when the tax gatherer is not put out of countenance by genius the surplus might well be left in the empty coffers of the orchestra. Fortunately, some of the leading conductors do good by stealth and reduce their fees considerably for an orchestra which has proved its own sincere qualities. But the broad fact remains. When it has been said that, for box-office purposes, 'the only artist worth engaging is the one you can't afford,' the absurdity of it all will be realized.

While this remains true, the young conductor will wait indefinitely for his opportunities. As soon as the public, which controls the box-office, gains a sense of musical proportion something better may be done. A series of concerts at a reasonable fee will bring the young man a greater reward than a single exaggerated engagement; it will give him the thing he needs most – an orchestra with whom he can work and try his skill, and whose players will train him as rapidly as he trains them.

With the problem of the young conductor goes that of the young composer, who is, indeed, in an even more frustrating position. The increase in orchestral activities since the war has done relatively little for him. Apart from a few enterprising festivals which commission or at least perform novelties, he is almost banished from our programmes. Perhaps it is that the new public has yet to satiate itself with the established masterpieces before it will accept the risk of deciding for itself; perhaps our composers have lost touch with the musical minds of the people; perhaps our musical planners have lost their enterprise. Few people would dare to put forward a final answer.

There have been many suggestions of cures, going as far as demanding that the Arts Council, responsible for granting money to orchestras, should insist on the performance of new works by the orchestral recipients. This has been the practice in France, with results which bring the whole matter into question. Ingenious schemes are put forward of playing a new work without mentioning it in advance publicity, thus avoiding frightening the public away. And yet the problem remains.

An orchestral council, co-ordinating the work of all our orchestras, might well find an answer, even if it were no more than a decree that so many performances a year be devoted to British works. It cannot be doubted that the stimulus of orchestral concerts and increased opportunities of hearing his own works frequently performed would encourage many a young and gifted composer to surpass anything which has been possible up to the present. It is a comfortable thought for us to imagine that composers are fed by their inspirations and that, providing the gifts are there, the music will follow. We fail to see that musical composition is a craft like any other, that it is one which cannot be satisfactorily carried on in the tranquillity of a study, however frequently visited by the Muse. The greatest music in the orchestral repertory has been the work of men who have spent their lives in touch with an orchestra, experimenting, testing the products of their gifted imagination against the hard facts of the orchestral result until they had acquired a mastery of their material and of their medium. We could safely anticipate a renaissance of musical composition to follow an extensive national plan for orchestral music.

Vocal and instrumental soloists from our own country have derived some benefit from the greater number of symphony orchestras and concerts. They have, however, had to compete against the many soloists who have come from other countries, and opportunities are still limited. Of British soloists few are steadily in demand, and those who appear frequently have succeeded in raising their fees to unaccustomed levels. Those among them who are still willing to prepare new works, or to devote the time necessary to renew their art by rest and study, merit such increased rewards; but with the public demand restricted to a few well-known concertos or, for singers, a few hackneyed arias, and the easy satisfaction gained from popular acclamation and material prosperity, only too many artists soon come to regard earning a high income as the only reason for their work. Small wonder that their playing becomes stale, or their voices tired when they should have reached the height of their careers.

If the public were more discriminating and more curious, a demand for lesser-known works would be an unfailing incentive to soloists, the more so if our national council took steps to discipline those who disregarded so flagrantly their responsibilities. It may seem that I am unjust in these remarks, but when I mention a famous singer who, engaged to take part in the performance of an outstanding masterpiece under the direction of one of the world's greatest conductors, could not resist accepting another engagement in a distant town the night before, and left after the important occasion to travel overnight to yet another engagement, it will be agreed that something needs to be done. And the pianist who will accept a daily performance in different towns for long periods should, in his own interest, be persuaded to understand that the public deserves more than a mechanical repetition.

Many foreign artists have something unique to offer us, and are always welcome in our concert halls, but those who have settled in America have learned to charge fees which are crippling to any of our music societies. Certain of them demand more than £1000 for a single performance, a fee which, despite a magnificent audience, has no justification. A national organization, with its own booking facilities, could offer such soloists a series of appearances with several orchestras at an interesting but not exorbitant fee, earned without extra expense during a single visit. The best artists would be likely to accept; the others might be lost without too much regret. English musicians are generous, and seldom attempt to prevent foreign artists from visiting the country, unless the quality of the visitor is commonplace. Then they have a rough-and-ready arrangement with the Ministry of Labour to lodge any objections and justify them before appointed experts. This is not yet a wholly satisfactory screening, and needs to be dealt with in a more directly responsible manner.

If all this were done, our young soloists would be offered yet more scope, and might, with an organized international exchange, find opportunities abroad of a like nature.

Opera is one of the most dangerous and expensive words in the English language. Dangerous, because the mere mention of it in England will cause controversy and arouse latent feelings of condemnation and annoyance; expensive, because its history in this country has been an almost unbroken sequence of bankruptcies, culminating in that of the small company controlling the pre-war L.P.O. If all this gigantic expenditure had put opera on its feet, if anything approaching a national opera had come to pass, if even an appreciation of opera had been inculcated in the British public, not a penny would have been lost. All we had for our pains, however, until after World War II was the Sadler's Wells Opera, gallantly taking its wares round the country; but none of the money squandered was spent on that body.

Opera is, as a matter of fact, not solely a question of finance. Many other factors are involved and usually overlooked. To face them means admitting so much, and demands imagination and energy. In the first place, opera in England has always been an imported product; we have even boasted of that fact from the day when Covent Garden was called the Italian Opera to the recent International Grand Opera Season, when almost the only British contribution was the personnel of the orchestra, and an occasional conductor. The high, melodramatic notes of the Italian tenors and sopranos, the mad profundities of the Russian bass, or the turgid melancholy and gloom of so many German operas may have delighted the polyglot globe-trotters who frequented Covent Garden or Glyndebourne, but had little significance for the average Englishman who demands on the stage something which bears a relation to the life he is living, in a language he understands; for no amount of snobbish enthusiasm is going to convince him finally that to laugh at the instigation of the stalls is to be amused. Do not think that I am decrying the art of other countries. For those whom good fortune has made capable of appreciating them, the attempts to get opera going in this country, held back as they have been by the weight of social distinctions, have achieved a great deal; but since our concern now is with the realistic problem of establishing music in general, and opera in particular, on a sound, popular basis, we must leave all the specialist sides of musical life to the few people to whom they make an appeal.

At present, there is more hope for opera in Britain than ever before. Covent Garden, restored to its proper functions soon after the war, has already made strides towards establishing itself as a national opera house. Generously aided by the Arts Council it is gradually achieving a style of performance which, in spite of the faults inevitable in a country without a permanent opera tradition, promises well. It is easy for critics to compare it with their reminiscences of pre-war Grand Seasons when the finest singers of the world were brought over regardless of expense. But, important as is singing to opera, orchestral playing, general production, and chorus work have no less a part to play. Notwithstanding certain eccentricities, the level of work at Covent Garden has been creditable, and the unduly delayed invitations to such trainers as Erich Kleiber will accelerate developments.

The critics normally miss the point in their efforts to find fault with the present régime. They might be better employed if they were to examine the practical problems which ultimately cause the aesthetic weaknesses they deplore. When a new opera is mounted at the cost of

£10,000, and when, despite this luxury, it is inadequately rehearsed when the first night arrives, and where leading figures behind the production are at loggerheads, something is wrong. The more so when the opera fails and is withdrawn after a handful of performances.

Enormous production costs may be part and parcel of the film world, where the value of a film depends largely on what it costs, but in the more genuinely artistic field of opera other values must be sought. Covent Garden yields too much to pre-war snobbishness, and attempts to recapture the false glories of that era. Its much-trumpeted extravagances are often put quietly to shame by its poorer and more modest neighbour of Rosebery Avenue. Sadler's Wells has achieved the highest quality of work, notably in *Simone Boccanegra* and *The School for Fathers*, with neither the money nor famous names demanded in Long Acre. Teamwork and artistic standards have outstripped, as they always will, the ease of wealth and cosmopolitanism.

Yet, apart from the Carl Rosa Company, the promising attempt to build a national opera in Wales, and the annual excursion from Covent Garden, Britain has little opera. The orchestra is the crux of the problem, for a touring company has had to choose between the horrors of a scratch orchestra gathered together in each town, or the uneconomic cost of touring a large body of players. With an efficient orchestra already established in many centres, needing the encouragement of a period of guaranteed work each year, some co-operation between opera and symphony orchestras might have been expected. Instead, we have had competition. Covent Garden opera descends on a provincial town, often with little or no warning, and gives performances which clash with concerts arranged months earlier. And both organizations depend on Government grants! This folly illustrates once more the need for national planning.

There is encouraging evidence that a taste for opera could be rapidly developed throughout the country, and although the tradition of a mainly foreign opera must persist for some time, British opera could soon establish itself. Several operas by our own composers, completed recently, have every claim to be staged. With this encouragement we could look forward to a day when opera will be as indigenous here as it is in Italy, Germany, or France. But simpler, less costly productions alone can make this progress possible.

If composers turned their talents in this direction, reactions in other sections of the musical world would be no less important. I have already spoken of the difficulties facing young singers and conductors, difficulties which rob us of much talent and energy. Here, in opera, would be an almost unlimited field of work and experience, a searching ground for quality, and a laboratory for refining it. A conductor who has been through the mill of opera, and one need only name Mahler, Toscanini, Beecham, Bruno Walter, and Victor de Sabata, would be thoroughly equipped in technique and experience, accustomed to the handling of an orchestra, a chorus, and solo singers, and with a wealth of human experience behind him. For the singers themselves untold opportunities would be presented, and there is no reason to doubt that the qualities which have gone to the making of many a fine English choir would reach a higher stage and produce a healthy native school of opera singing.

*

Of orchestral playing itself, the crux of the whole matter, little more need be said. The fact that, in spite of enormous difficulties, little and spasmodic encouragement, an entire lack of co-operation with the schools of music, and a profound feeling of inferiority due to a conviction that we belong to an unmusical nation, we have been able to build up so many admirable orchestral organizations suggests if it does not prove the great potentialities which we possess. That conditions in which these gifts may be allowed to mature more favourably can be found is the belief that has gone to the writing of this book. A great deal of dead wood, hard prejudice, and time-honoured misconceptions has to be cleared away before any substantial progress is made; we must be willing to recognize, even though it breaks the narrow circle of our privileged intellectual position, that music is an art for all, and that without the enthusiasm and support of an immense and constant public all our ambitions will fall to the ground. Subsidies for orchestras, schools for orchestral players, opportunities for conductors and soloists, will have no meaning beyond preciosity if they are not regarded as a means to that end, and if they are considered otherwise than in relation to the wide demand of a national need.

It is not enough for a country to produce a star conductor, an international tenor, or a world-famous fiddler; we have allowed all, or nearly all, our sporting championships to go abroad, and although we may feel a twinge at the knowledge of our individual inferiority in such matters as tennis, cricket, swimming, horse-jumping, and so on, we are more than reassured by the fact that, the stars apart, the average standard at such pursuits is as high or higher in England than elsewhere. And so, with our musical organization we must aim at a high common standard, and not be content to know that there may be first-class symphony concerts in the new hall, expensive opera at Covent Garden, and music elsewhere in a few centres. That we should have all these things is right, for the standard must be upheld, but they must be no more than the high lights of a musical life which, spread thoroughly over the country, will have become no less an integral part of our life than books, the cinema, football matches, and sport generally. But while all these admirable enterprises are uncoordinated, while their economies are secured only from year to year, they are perpetually threatened by those who control our musical life without understanding it.

The schemes and ideas which I have tentatively put forward in this and foregoing chapters are, of course, part of a long-term policy, and not every detail could become practical politics at this moment. But the progress made in the first five years of a precarious peace demonstrates the musical capacity of our country. Another five years uninterrupted by war, and less precarious as they then might be, would astonish us all. If the élan of victory has long since lost its force, if the cost of international misunderstanding directs economy at our cultural work, and if doubt has replaced confidence and optimism, we must not therefore resign from our tasks. Our art is the strongest sanity in a world of imaginary fears, where the enjoyment of life has been forgotten. We must demand against all other claims the means to continue along our developing path. Here we are, a nation once derided for its lack of musical powers, with a living school of composers unsurpassed anywhere; with a ballet comparable with the best in existence; with orchestras we are proud to send abroad, and choirs worth making long journeys to hear. Are we to let them languish, these arts of peace, while all our thoughts are turned to destruction?

We are faced with a double struggle: to eliminate all that leads to a belief that wars follow peace as night follows day, and at the same time to preserve those values which some leaders would scrap in a misguided confidence in material powers. But the immensity of all that is at stake, the vision of all that may be lost, is awakening thousands of people to a recognition of the treasures they possess. Music offers them relaxation, renewed strength, a touchstone to show they are truly alive, a reassurance that the future can be wide enough to hold their hopes.

If our musical future has been never more promising, it has been never more in danger. We must build and build, preserve what we have inherited and establish it upon a foundation that will withstand the unimagined shocks to come, upon a foundation not of stone but of strong roots, the roots of a tree which may bend and shake, but which will endure and spread its branches, giving shelter and refreshment to humanity throughout the ages.

Index

America
  development of orchestral music
    in, 24
  scope for talent, 66, 189
  subsidies for orchestra, 166, 173
Amsterdam, Concertgebouw, 113
Applause, 137 ff.
Apprenticeships for players, 92
Army bands, 108
Arne, Thomas, 24
Arts Council of Great Britain, 17,
  123, 181 ff., 192, 196
Auditions, 84 ff.

'B's, the three, 131
Bach, Johann Sebastian, 144
Bach-Handel period, 69
Balakirev, Mily, 74
Barbirolli, Sir John, 64, 66, 79,
  132, 188
Bayreuth, influence of, 141
B.B.C.
  accent and pronunciation, 70
  adoption of Proms by, 51
  announcer and the ghost, 158
  cause of increased demand for
    symphony concerts, 184
  one of its finest achievements,
    173
  orchestral players as artists, 93
  patronage of music, 150, 166
  provincial orchestras, 65
B.B.C. Symphony Orchestra, 34,
  84, 110, 111
Beard, Paul, 51
Beecham, Sir Thomas
  and creditors, 36

Beecham, Sir Thomas – contd
  and disappointed soloists, 87
  and opera, 198
  and the L.S.O., 34
  climax of career, 35
  criticism of City Hall, Sheffield,
    121
  dissimilarity from other conduc-
    tors, 188
  exquisite phrasing, 60
  failure to appear, 51
  gramophone recordings, 153, 155
  inheritance, genius, hard work,
    66
  makes an appeal, 173
  necessity for an audience, 133
  on mutilation of masterpieces, 74,
    75
  opera rehearsal, 55, 56
  philistine audiences, 138
  reaction to war-time committee,
    37
  Toscanini and – , truly great, 62
Beecham and Pharaoh, 39
Beethoven, Ludwig van, 23
  Second Symphony, slow move-
    ment, 155
  Fifth Symphony, 23, 116, 126
  Seventh Symphony, 129
  Ninth (Choral) Symphony, 28,
    116
  Violin Concerto, 153
  and patrons, 145, 146
  Philharmonic Society of London,
    25
  reaction to music of, 128
  reception of musical ideas, 69
Beinum, Eduard van, 60

Belle Vue, Manchester, 120
Bergmann, Robert, 70
Berlin, City of, 31
  L.P.O. visit, 31
  Philharmonic Orchestra, 30 ff., 85, 114
Berlioz, Hector, 23, 74
  Harold in Italy, 104
  Marche au Supplice, 151
  Symphonie Fantastique, 151
  breadth of cultural outlook, 102
  memoirs of, 68
  remarks on incomplete orchestration, 68 ff.
Birmingham Symphony Orchestra, City of, 182, 186
Bolshoi Theatre, 47
Borsdorf, Adolf, 108, 149
Boult, Sir Adrian, 132, 188
Bournemouth Municipal Orchestra, 182
Brahms, Johannes, 70, 114
  Violin Concerto, 153
Brailsford, H. N., 43
Bristol Colston Hall, 120
Brodsky, Adolf, 30
Bruckner, Anton, 132
Burns, Robert, 126
Busoni, Ferruccio, 102
Byrd, William, 143

Cameron, Basil, 52, 64, 66
Carl Rosa Company, 197
C.E.M.A., 181
Central Halls, 121, 123
Chamber music, 96
Chapel Royal, 143 ff., 148
Charles II, 144
Chatham, Central Hall, 171
Chopin, Frédéric, 152
Church, music in the service of the, 143
Churchill, Winston, 126
City Hall, Sheffield, 121
City of Birmingham Symphony Orchestra, 182, 186

Cinemas, 121
Civic Halls, 122
Cockerill
  family, 109
  John, 110
  Winifred, 110
Colston Hall, Bristol, 120
Concertgebouw, Amsterdam, 113
Concertgebouw Orchestra, 113
Conductor
  essential qualifications of, 56, 57
  need of, 44 ff.
Costa, Michael, 49
Costs of provincial tours, 168, 169
Couperin, François, 144
Covent Garden Opera, 197
  Royal Opera House, 26, 36, 38, 48, 66, 195, 196, 199
Cremona, 21
Cruft, Eugene, 106
Culture of players, 98
Cundell, Eric, 63

Davies, W. H., 125
Davis Cinema, Croydon, 121
Debussy, Claude, 70
Delius, Frederick, 74
Deputy system, 32 ff., 81

England
  art of music in, 149
  middle-class musicians, 148
England and Germany
  comparison of concert halls, 120
  comparison of scope for musicians, 147

Fauré, Gabriel, *Requiem*, 171
Festival of Britain, 117
Fokine, Michel, 141
Fox, Sir Cyril, 122
France, 148
Free Trade Hall, Manchester, 120
Furtwängler, Dr Wilhelm, 85

Germany
  audiences in, 140
  private patrons, 24, 146, 147
  respect for orchestral musicians,
    26
  story of viola player, 96
Gershwin, George, *Rhapsody in Blue*,
  125
Gewandhaus, Leipzig, 26, 27, 113
Glyndebourne, 195
Goethe, 146
Gogh, Vincent van, 84
Goossens
  Eugène, 64, 66, 149
  family, 109
  Marie, 109
  Sidonie, 109
Gramophone recording, 156, 157

Hadow, Sir Charles, 145
Hallé magazine, 14
Hallé Orchestra, 17, 30, 79, 110,
  120, 132, 182, 186
  Sir Charles, 29, 30
  Society, 30
Handel, Frederick, 24, 145, 148
  Grand Commemoration of, 48
  musician to Elector of Hanover,
    144
  pensions from Queen Anne and
    George I, 144
Harrison, Julius, 22
Harty, Sir Hamilton, 30, 188
Haydn, Franz Josef, 22, 145
Heifetz, Jascha, 153
Hess, Dame Myra, 179
Hess, Willy, 30
Heward, Leslie, 30, 188
Hieronymus, Archbishop, 145
Hitler, Adolf, 26, 31

Incorporated Society of Musicians, 146
Infant prodigies, 58, 102

International Grand Opera season,
  195
Italian operas, 139, 195
Iturbi, José, 54

Jeunesses Musicales, 165
Johnson, Dr 126

Kienzl, Wilhelm, 102
Kleiber, Erich, 196
Koussevitzky, Serge, 47, 188
Kralik, Heinrich von, 28
Krehbiel, Henry Edward, 28
Kreisler, Fritz, 153, 154

Lasso, Orlando di, 143
Liszt, Abbé Franz, 102, 147
Liverpool Council, rebuke to
  Liverpool Philharmonic Society,
  29
Liverpool Philharmonic Hall, 29,
  120
  Philharmonic Orchestra, 182,
    186
  Philharmonic Society, 28
London Concerts Co-ordination
  Association, 183
London County Council, 17, 94
  concerts for children, 163
  plan for South Bank develop-
    ment, 117
London Philharmonic Orchestra
  advice on lay-out of Royal
    Festival Hall, 118
  an artistic republic, 178
  and Beecham, 35
  and conductors, 42
  and Richard Tauber, 100
  and society, 82
  concert in Blackpool, 125
  dilemma – 1939, 158
  emphasis on team-work, 79
  financial collapse, 36

Index

London Philharmonic Orchestra—
contd
  financial crises, 173
  gramophone recordings with
    Heifetz and Kreisler, 153
  horn quartet, 108
  interests represented by the
    N.A.S.O., 182
  journal of the, see Philharmonic
    Post
  leader as conductor, 51
  London's permanent orchestra,
    76
  loyalty of players, 98
  mistakes of first six months, 174
  musicians from the Hallé, 30
  new régime, 36 ff.
  opera financially disastrous, 195
  pensions fund, 94
  provincial concerts, 131, 132
  provincial concerts for children,
    162
  recording of horn passage, 155
  revelation of unusual talent, 91
  self-government, 42, 181
  successor to the R.P.O., 167
  talents and hobbies, 111
  war-time recovery, 179
  women orchestral players, 110
London Symphony Observer, 14
London Symphony Orchestra
  formation of, 34, 146
  interests represented by the
    N.A.S.O., 182
  orchestral committee, 108
  resilience of, 179
  revolutionary development, 36
Long playing records, 159
Lotter, Adolf, 106
Louis XIV, 144, 166
Ludwig, King of Bavaria, 147
Lully, Jean Baptiste, 144, 166

Mahler, Gustav, 132, 198
Malko, Nicolai, 47

Manchester
  Belle Vue, 120
  Free Trade Hall, 120
  R.C.M., 30
Massine, Leonide, 141
Mayer, Dr Wilhelm, 102 (see also
    Rémy, W. A.)
Mayer, Sir Robert, 161
Mendelssohn, Felix, 70, 114, 172
  Midsummer Night's Dream Scherzo,
    42
Menuhin, Yehudi, 102
Mercadante, 148
Methodist Central Halls, 121, 123
Moscow, 43, 45 ff.
Moussorgsky, Modeste Petrovich
  Boris Godunov, 73
  A Night on the Bare Mountain, 74
Mozart, Wolfgang Amadeus, 23
  attitude to patronage, 145, 146
Musical Companion, The, 22
Musical Times, The, 104
Musicians' Union, 91, 97, 146,
    158, 170
Music Development Committee
  of the, 185, 187

National Association of Sym-
    phony Orchestras, 182
National Gallery, 84, 179
National Museum of Wales, 122
National Orchestra of Wales, 185,
    186
Nazi Government, 31
Newman, Ernest, 54, 104
New York Philharmonic, 27, 28
New York Symphony Orchestra,
    28
Nicolai, Carl Otto, 28, 94
  concert, 28, 94
Nikisch, Arthur, 64, 114
Nottingham, splendid audience,
    171

Opera, 195 ff.

Orchestral Employers' Association, 183

Orchestral players, spare-time pursuits, 110 ff.

Paganini, Niccolo, 104, 153
Palestrina, Giovanni Pierluigi da, 143
Patronage, 143 ff.
Pensions for players, 93, 94
Performing Right Society, 133
Permanent orchestra, positive advantages of, 76 ff.
Petri, Egon, 46, 154
Pettit, Walter, 148
Pezze, Signor, 148
Philharmonic Hall, Liverpool, 29, 120
Philharmonic Post, The, 14, 112
Philharmonic Society of London
and L.P.O. pensions fund, 94
and the Ninth Symphony, 27, 28
as patron, 166
concert programmes, 49
English orchestral players, 148
foremost connexion with Beethoven, 25
formation of, 24
gold medal of, 25
historic opportunity missed, 26
Philharmonie, Berlin, 28, 114
Players
apprenticeships for, 92
auditions of, 84 ff.
general culture of, 98
pensions for, 93, 94
recommendation of, 84
Preparation of students, 90, 91
Priestley, J. B., 39, 173
Proms, 51, 114, 116, 117, 130, 148
Provincial tours, costs of, 168, 169
Prussia, State of, 31
Puccini, Giacomo, *La Bohème*, 55
Purcell, Henry, 23, 144

Queen's Hall, 33, 34, 52, 64, 114, 116, 117
Orchestra, 114

Radio Times, The, 43
Rameau, Jean Philippe, 144
Ravel, Maurice, *Boléro*, 126
Recommendation of players, 84
Reformation, 143
Rémy, W. A., 102, 103 (*see also* Mayer, Dr Wilhelm)
Reznicek, Emil Nicolaus von, 102
Richter, Hans, 30, 64
Rimsky-Korsakov, Nicholas, 23, 74
Coq d'Or, 63
Royal Albert Hall, 52, 83, 114 ff., 130, 138, 170
Royal Festival Hall, 117, 170
Royal Opera House, Covent Garden, 26, 36, 38, 48, 66, 195, 196, 199
Royal Philharmonic Orchestra, 37, 167
Royal Philharmonic Society, *see* Philharmonic Society of London

Sabata, Victor de, 60, 198
Sadler's Wells, 66, 195, 197
Sargent, Sir Malcolm, children's concerts, 161, 164
Scarlatti, Alessandro, 144
Schnabel, Artur, 154
School for Fathers, The, 197
Schubert, Franz
Symphony in C major, 73
Unfinished Symphony, 129
Schumann, Robert, 73, 114
Scottish National Orchestra, 120, 182, 185
Shakespeare, 59, 126, 161
Shaw, George Bernard, 62
Sheffield, City Hall, 121
Shore, Bernard, 104

Index

Sibelius, Jan, 166, 185
  Violin Concerto, 153
Simone Boccanegra, 197
Smyth, Dame Ethel, 39
Southampton Civic Hall, 122
Spohr, Ludwig, 46, 49
Stanley, Mr, 148
Strauss, Richard, 23
  Don Quixote, 104
  Heldenleben, 50
Students, preparation of, 90, 91
Symphony Orchestra, 18
Szell, George, 154

Tallis, Thomas, 143
Tate Gallery, 84
Tauber, Richard, 100
Tchaikovsky, Peter Ilyich
  Francesca da Rimini, 55
  Fourth Symphony, 73
  Fifth Symphony, 73
Tchehov, Anton, 94
Tertis, Lionel, 104, 153
Toscanini, Arturo, 60, 62, 64, 70, 71, 188, 191, 198
Tseitlin, Lev, 47

U.S.S.R., 46

Vaughan Williams, Ralph, 188
  London Symphony, 171

Vienna Philharmonic Orchestra, 27, 28, 94, 178
Vinci, Leonardo da, 100

Wagner, Richard, 23, 102, 109, 147
  Parsifal, 139
Walter, Bruno, 60, 198
Walthamstow Civic Hall, 122
Watford Civic Hall, 122
Weber, Carl Maria von, 140
  Invitation to the Waltz, 139
Weelkes, Thomas, 143
Weimar, 147
Weimar Republic, 31
Weingartner, Felix, 101, 102
  Buffets and Rewards, 147
Wembley Civic Hall, 122
Wolverhampton Civic Hall, 122
Women in orchestras, 110
Wood, Sir Henry, 52
  and deputy system, 33
  and formation of L.S.O., 34
  and Lev Tseitlin, 47
  and Proms, 117, 130
  attention to details, 50
  dissimilarity from other conductors, 188
  inspired indefatigability of, 130
  perseverance and encouragement, 149
  respect for composer's work, 71
  women orchestral players, 110
Woodhouse, Charles, 51